OSPREY AIRCRAFT OF THE ACES • 98

Spitfire Aces of North Africa and Italy

SERIES EDITOR: TONY HOLMES

OSPREY AIRCRAFT OF THE ACES • 98

Spitfire Aces of North Africa and Italy

Andrew Thomas

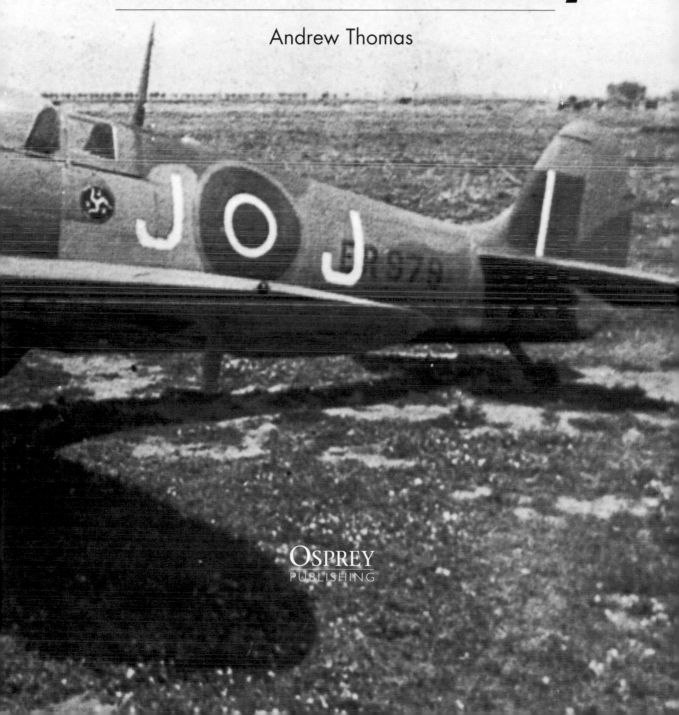

OSPREY
PUBLISHING

Front Cover
By mid-April 1943 Axis forces in North Africa were trapped into a shrinking area of Tunisia, surrounded by the Allies to the south, east and west and the Mediterranean to the north. In order to reinforce and resupply the German and Italian troops, the enemy began an airlift across the Mediterranean that involved large numbers of transport aircraft drawn from both the Luftwaffe and the *Regia Aeronautica*. To interdict this air bridge the Allies commenced Operation *Flax*, which saw RAF and USAAF fighters flying sweeps off the North African coast that were to reap a rich harvest.

Despite having suffered severe losses, the transport squadrons were determined to keep flying resupply missions to the forces cut off in Tunisia. Early on the morning of 22 April another formation set out from Sicily. Shortly after 0700 hrs a dozen Spitfire VCs of No 1 Sqn South African Air Force (SAAF), led by the CO, Maj D D 'Snowy' Moodie, with a top cover of six Polish Spitfires from No 145 Sqn, took off as escorts for USAAF P-40 Warhawks of the 79th Fighter Group. The Spitfires spotted a formation of Allied fighters off the coast and headed out over the Gulf of Tunis. Unknowingly, they had picked up a SAAF Kittyhawk wing rather than the Americans!

Ten miles off the coast near the island of Zembra, in a slight mist over a perfectly calm Mediterranean, a formation of six-engined Me 323s flying in a large vic of 15, with a smaller vic of five inside them, was spotted heading for Tunis. They had an escort of ten Bf 109s and C.202s. Realising that the Kittyhawks had not seen them, Maj Moodie ordered 'Green' and 'Red' sections to attack. Within minutes a great slaughter had commenced off Cape Bon.

Diving on the transports was Lt 'Robbie' Robinson in Spitfire VC JG959/AX-N. He was in turn attacked by the fighter escorts;

'I peeled off, and only when diving down did I see the escorting '109s behind and above the transports. Two of these pulled up and I followed, giving the No 2 a deflection burst. I out-climbed the No 2, and from time to time opened fire, closing from 100 yards to 30 yards. The long-range tank burst into flames and fell away. I gave the '109 further bursts although he was alight. When I broke

away he was going down in flames.'

Lt D M Brebner saw the fighter crash into the sea, thus giving the 24-year-old ace status. Robinson was not finished, however;

'I climbed up over the same area and saw more '109s climbing up slightly ahead of me. I gained on the No 2 in a pair and gave him four bursts, the first at about 200 yards and the last at 50 yards. I saw strikes all over the '109, pieces flying off the machine, and as it rolled over on its back it was belching a huge column of black smoke and it went straight down.'

Once again, Brebner saw his victim crash. Robinson concluded;

'I was attacked many times, as my No 2 had got separated from me. Eventually, a Kitty Hawk joined me and acted as my No 2. We were attacked by four '109s, and I got off a burst of machine gun fire, my cannon

ammo being exhausted, but observed no results.'

Robinson's victims were probably the Bf 109s of Unteroffizier Heinz Gollitz, who failed to return, and Leutnant Schlechter who was shot down into the sea but rescued. Both pilots were from of 6./JG 27.

By 0850 hrs the massacre of the Me 323s was over, with 14 having been claimed destroyed, as well as several of their escorts. It was reported that Field Marshal Albert Kesselring, commander of all German land and air forces in the Mediterranean, was aghast when informed of these losses, and he ordered that all daylight air convoys be stopped immediately.

This specially commissioned artwork by Mark Postlethwaite shows Robinson closing on his first victim just as the Bf 109's long-range tank burst into flames

First published in Great Britain in 2011 by Osprey Publishing
Midland House, West Way, Botley, Oxford, OX2 0PH
44-02 23rd Street, Suite 219, Long Island City, NY, 11101, USA

E-mail; info@ospreypublishing.com

ISBN 13; 978 1 84908 343 0
E-book ISBN: 978 1 84908 344 7

Edited by Tony Holmes
Page design by Tony Truscott
Cover Artwork by Mark Postlethwaite
Aircraft Profiles by Chris Davey
Index by Alan Thatcher
Originated by United Graphics Pte
Printed and bound in China through Bookbuilders

11 12 13 14 15   10 9 8 7 6 5 4 3 2 1

Osprey Publishing is supporting the Woodland Trust, the UK's leading woodland conservation charity by funding the dedication of trees.

www.ospreypublishing.com

CONTENTS

CHAPTER 1
SPITFIRES OVER THE SANDS 6

CHAPTER 2
EL ALAMEIN AND BEYOND   9

CHAPTER 3
***TORCH* TO TUNIS 23**

CHAPTER 4
ACROSS THE MEDITERRANEAN 47

CHAPTER 5
ITALY – THE LONG FLOG 58

CHAPTER 6
**OVER THE AEGEAN AND
THE BALKANS 78**

CHAPTER 7
VICTORY! 83

APPENDICES 86
COLOUR PLATES COMMENTARY 89
INDEX 95

SPITFIRES OVER THE SANDS

'**S**pitfires made ten sorties acting as high cover to Hurricanes. Flt Lt Sabourin and Sgt James attacked two ME 109s southwest of Tobruk. One ME 109 destroyed.'

Thus in the dry and prosaic language of the handwritten Operational Record Book (ORB) of No 145 Sqn for 8 June 1942 did the diarist record the first victory of a Spitfire over the Western Desert. Joseph Sabourin, a 27-year-old Canadian who already had three victories to his name from flying Tomahawks with No 112 Sqn, and his wingman Sgt James had shot down a Bf 109 over the desert some 15 miles to the southwest of Tobruk. Sabourin had scrambled from Gambut at the controls of Spitfire VB AB321/ZX-N at 1600 hrs, with his wingman flying AB324/ZX-A, and they had landed back just 50 minutes later.

Eight days earlier the same pair had given the Spitfire its baptism of fire over the desert when at dusk on 1 June, as the Battle of Gazala raged, No 145 Sqn flew its first Spitfire mission. Having been scrambled, Sabourin and James had damaged a Ju 88 conducting a reconnaissance mission near Gambut. This event was also prosaically recorded;

'Flt Lt Sabourin and Sgt James patrolled Gambut to intercept an enemy reconnaissance aircraft. This aircraft came over every day, always varying the time it came. No interception was made. At 1745 hrs they took off again and damaged a Ju 88.'

With the Luftwaffe achieving a degree of ascendancy over the RAF's Hurricanes, Tomahawks and Kittyhawks in North Africa by early 1942, the despatch of squadrons of the iconic and capable Spitfire to Egypt was seen as a matter of urgency, despite demands elsewhere. No 145 Sqn was an experienced unit within Fighter Command, and in mid-February 1942 it had left for the Middle East together with another experienced Spitfire squadron, No 92. Pilots of the latter disembarked at Takoradi, in West Africa, to ferry aircraft up to Cairo, and they eventually reassembled with the unit's ground party in April.

The end of April also saw No 601 Sqn arrive in Egypt, having come via Malta, and it too began readying itself for renewed operations. By then No 145 Sqn had begun to receive its Spitfire VBs at Helwan, on the Nile south of Cairo, where it had worked up as part of the Western Desert Air Force (WDAF). These machines were the

Flying Spitfire VB AB326/ZX-A on 1 June 1942, Flt Lt Joseph Sabourin of No 145 Sqn attacked and damaged a Ju 88 that was conducting a reconnaissance mission near Gambut. This was the first air combat for the Spitfire over the desert (*D R Neate*)

Canadian Flt Lt Joseph Sabourin participated in the first two Spitfire combats over the desert and shared in the fighter's first victory – over a Bf 109 – on 8 June 1942. He shot down another Messerschmitt fighter on the 12th to become the first pilot to achieve acedom in North Africa when flying a Spitfire (*via L Milberry*)

Flt Lt Sabourin's wingman Sgt James was flying AB324/ZX-L when he shared in the first two Spitfire claims over the desert on 1 and 8 June. This aircraft was also flown by Sabourin on a patrol the day after he achieved ace status (*F Twitchett*)

first Spitfires in the Middle East. By now, Generalfeldmarschall Erwin Rommel's *Afrika Korps* and his Italian allies had been steadily building up against the Allied front in Cyrenaica that ran from Gazala south through Bir Hacheim. On 24 May No 145 Sqn had moved forward to Gambut, between Tobruk and Bardia, and commenced flying defensive patrols. Two days later Rommel attacked Gazala, thus beginning six weeks of violent fighting on the ground and in the air that was eventually to result in a British retreat deep into Egypt.

Initially, No 145 Sqn was restricted to defensive patrols from Gambut. Indeed, because of a shortage of aircraft on 2 June Sqn Ldr Jeff Wedgewood and a dozen of his No 92 Sqn pilots began a temporary attachment to Hurricane II-equipped No 80 Sqn, where they gained a number of successes.

The enemy thrust deep into the south to bypass the Gazala defences and struck against Bir Hacheim, where Maj Gen Marie Pierre Koenig's 1st Free French Brigade gallantly stood fast for 16 days against massive enemy pressure. The heavy fighting led to No 145 Sqn's Spitfires seeing more action in defence of the fort, with engagements overhead Bir Hacheim reaching their climax on 10 June. That morning, while providing top cover for Hurricanes, No 145 Sqn CO Sqn Ldr Charles Overton succeeded in downing ace Oberleutnant Rudolf Sinner, *Staffelkapitän* of 6./JG 27. This proved to be Overton's only victory in the desert, taking his tally to 5.5 destroyed.

Two days later, despite heavy sandstorms, the fighting continued. That evening Overton's squadron was scrambled to meet a large inbound raid of Ju 87s and Ju 88s, escorted by 18 Bf 109s. To the south of Tobruk near El Adem, Joseph Sabourin (on this occasion flying AB329/ZX-M) shot down a Bf 109F, thought to have been 'Yellow 9' of 9./JG 53 flown

by Feldwebel Heinz Herkenhoff, who was killed. The Canadian thus became the first pilot to 'make ace' over North Africa in a Spitfire.

However, the situation on the ground continued to deteriorate, with the British suffering heavy losses at Knightsbridge. Soon afterwards they began a withdrawal from the Gazala line, resulting in DAF squadrons 'leapfrogging' in an easterly direction. The unit flew intensively throughout, completing some 22 sorties on the 16th. No 145 Sqn's diarist recorded the intensity of the air action the following day, as the battle reached its zenith;

'Standing patrols over base were resumed and 18 sorties were made. Plt Off Weber encountered a Macchi 202 near Gambut and pursued it to Sidi Rezegh. Near Amud he saw two ME 109s and fired at them, but did not see the result. Plt Off Hanley and Sgt Barker attacked two ME 109s and Flt Lt Monk and Plt Off Malins attacked two others. Plt Off Hanley and Sgt Barker provided a most inspiring spectacle as they chased the two MEs at a low altitude away from the aerodrome. The standing patrol was ended at 1705 hrs. The squadron left Gambut at 2100 hrs. At 2200 hrs we arrived at Sidi Azeiz satellite.

'It is not possible to know how many enemy aircraft were destroyed by the squadron. Three ME 109s and one Ju 88 were confirmed destroyed and three ME 109s and two Ju 88s were damaged. None of our aircraft received damage from the enemy. The moral effect of the squadron's operations was considerable, and it was felt respectively by the enemy and the units we operated with against him. It was a new experience for Messerschmitt pilots to have to look up instead of down!'

Despite much gallant fighting, the enemy's inexorable advance continued, and on the 21st Tobruk, so long a symbol of dogged resistance, surrendered. Its loss was a huge blow to Allied morale. This success prompted Rommel to continue his advance into Egypt, but during the day No 145 Sqn suffered its first Spitfire losses when Sgts Mahady and Bailey were shot down by Bf 109s of I./JG 27.

On 25 June, No 601 Sqn, now fully operational once more, moved forward to LG 13 in the desert to the southeast of Maaten Bagush and began flying missions two days later in company with No 145 Sqn. By month-end, the Allied forces were firmly entrenched on the El Alamein line, and the Spitfire had become established in the skies over the desert. Then, on 1 July, Rommel began his assault on the El Alamein defences.

The second Spitfire unit to become operational in the desert was No 601 Sqn, to which ER502/UF-X, belonged. This aircraft was issued to the unit in late 1942, and it was flown on occasion by New Zealand ace 21-year-old Flg Off Bruce Ingram. In contravention of regulations, the Auxiliary unit wore its badge on the tail. ER502 failed to return from a mission on 16 April 1943 (via B Cull)

EL ALAMEIN AND BEYOND

The assault on the Alamein Line resulted in further heavy fighting, but after heavy losses Rommel gave up his assault on 4 July. However, the bitter struggle for the control of the skies continued, with the relatively few Spitfires in-theatre being increasingly used to give roving high cover for other fighters performing strafing missions and formations of medium bombers whose attacks had proven so effective, earning them the name *'Hollenhunds'* ('Hellhounds') from the enemy.

Sadly, the following morning, having taken off on a patrol at 1045 hrs, No 145 Sqn's Sgt James reported that he was short of oxygen and he was never seen again. Later, in mid afternoon, the unit was in action once again when eight aircraft tangled with Bf 109s of II./JG 27, losing Flt Lt Monk. The following day a trio of Spitfires from No 601 Sqn took off and found their first action when, near Aboukir, they intercepted what was identified as an Me 210. The CO, Sqn Ldr John Bisdee, damaged the aircraft, this being the last of the ten-victory ace's claims. The squadron was in action again the next day when four pilots tangled with Bf 109s from III./JG 53 that were escorting some Ju 88s. The Spitfires were in turn jumped, resulting in Flt Lt Hagger and WO Belcher becoming the squadron's first casualties in the desert.

Nos 145 and 601 Sqns were not the only Spitfires in action, however, for to counter intrusions by very high flying Ju 86P reconnaissance aircraft, several fighters had been modified to intercept them by the High Altitude Flight of No 103 Maintenance Unit (MU) at Aboukir. The unit had several successful pilots among its number, including Plt Off Eric 'Jumbo' Genders, who during 1941 had shot down 7.5 enemy aircraft. He joined the High Altitude Flight, recalling in a letter;

'About June 1942 the Germans started to send high-flying Ju 86 photographic aircraft over our lines at intervals of about one a week. We started to go after these, but found that the ordinary Spitfire could not reach the necessary altitude. It was only when we used specially lightened Spitfires with "hotted-up" engines that we were able to get anywhere near the high-flyer. Even then, we were handicapped by not having pressure cabins, and we frequently suffered from the bends (the deep sea divers' disease) and the cold. However, the thrill of reaching these altitudes compensated for the discomforts.'

Genders' first encounter with the enemy came on 26 June when he damaged a Ju 86P, a feat that he repeated the next day.

Action over the frontline continued unabated, and an indication of the intensity of the fighting may be gained from the fact that on 11 July No 145 Sqn flew no fewer than eight escort missions. During the course of these missions two Bf 109s were claimed by Flg Off John Taylor (the first of his 15 victories) and Plt Off Eric Hanley (the first of his three

Having become an ace flying Hurricanes, in mid-1942 Plt Off 'Jumbo' Genders joined the High Altitude Flight of No 103 MU in Aboukir, where he made his final claims. Postwar, Genders became a test pilot, but he was killed flight-testing the DH 108 on 1 May 1950 (*No 33 Sqn Records*)

Spitfire VB BR114 was one of the aircraft modified at Aboukir for interception of the very high altitude Ju 86P reconnaissance flights over the Suez Canal. Heavily modified (and fitted with a four-bladed propeller), the fighter was regularly flown by Genders and future ace Plt Off Alastair Wilson (*A J Watton*)

Spitfire VC BR392/UF-P was one of the aircraft 'hijacked' in the Middle East when en route to Australia in mid-1942. It was flown by No 601 Sqn's youthful Bruce Ingram, who, on 7 September, shot down a Bf 109 of I./JG 27 to become the first pilot to claim five Spitfire victories in the desert campaign (*A Price*)

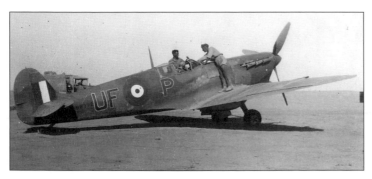

victories). Shortly after 1000 hrs on the 14th a four-aircraft section from No 601 Sqn took off on a freelance patrol during which Flt Lt Bruce Ingram and two others shared a Bf 109 to claim the squadron's first victory in the desert.

The fighting was far from one-sided though, as three days later a dozen Spitfires from No 145 Sqn that were covering a patrol of Hurricanes were jumped shortly after 0730 hrs by eight Bf 109s from II./JG 27 out on a *Frei Jagd*. Oberleutnant Sinner gained revenge for his shooting down by the squadron in June by hitting the Spitfire of Sgt Rostant, who was forced to bail out.

By now the *Afrika Korps* was exhausted and down to just 28 serviceable tanks, such were the depredations of Allied air attacks. Targets also included enemy airfields, with Fuka and El Daba being heavily hit on the 20th. The following day the 8th Army, under Gen Claude Auchinleck, launched a brief and abortive counter offensive, losing more than 100 tanks in just two days.

Early on the morning of 22 July six Spitfires from No 601 Sqn engaged a pair of Bf 109s and one of them, thought to have been flown by Oberleutnant Zahn, was shot down by Flt Lt Bruce Ingram, taking the 21-year-old New Zealander to acedom. A little later that morning a quartet from No 145 Sqn were covering Hurricanes when they were attacked by Bf 109s, and John Taylor's aircraft was hit in the cockpit and he was wounded in the head and neck. Plt Offs Frith and Laing-Meason both had to bail out, but not before the latter had claimed a probable – the first of his 13 claims, which included four victories.

Despite the ground fighting settling into an exhausted stalemate, the air fighting continued through the rest of the sweltering month and into August. On the 1st No 92 Sqn at last received its first Spitfire, establishing at LG 173 as part of No

244 Wing under Wg Cdr Love, joining Nos 145 and 601 Sqns. No 92 Sqn became operational on the 13th, flying its first Spitfire patrol the following day and ran into a big fight around a returning bomber formation. Appropriately, it was the CO, Sqn Ldr Jeff Wedgewood, who opened the unit's account in the desert by hitting the cooling system of the Bf 109 of II/JG 27's Leutnant Mix, who had to crash land and became a PoW.

Five days later on the 19th No 92 Sqn proved its worth when providing top cover to the Hurricanes of Nos 274 and 1 SAAF Sqns when, at 0915 hrs, the unit ran into a formation of Bf 109s and Macchi C.202s west of Hammam. The Spitfire pilots claimed several destroyed, including the C.202 of 73ª *Squadriglia*/9° *Gruppo* pilot Tenente Rinaldo Gibellini, which fell to Sqn Ldr Wedgewood. Among others that claimed was Canadian Plt Off 'Red' Chisholm, who destroyed a Bf 109F for the first of his seven Spitfire victories, and fellow future ace Sgt 'Sammy' Samouelle, who also claimed a Bf 109F before crash-landing.

Meanwhile, at Aboukir, success continued to evade the high-flying Spitfire VBs of No 103 MU despite the employment of heavily modified aircraft, so pilots revised their tactics by flying the intercepts in pairs rather than alone. This new approach was tried for the first time on 29 August when Plt Off Genders reached a firing position astern a Ju 86, although after a brief burst his guns jammed. Although he made no claim, the Junkers had indeed been badly hit and its crew was later forced to ditch in the Mediterranean. The No 103 MU pilots saw further action on the final day of the month when New Zealander Flt Lt Richard Webb attacked a Ju 88. Three days later, in concert with Sgt A McC Ross, he shot down an Italian bomber 70 miles west of Cairo, as he subsequently recalled;

'Attacked enemy aircraft, which was flying at 14,000 ft, from above and astern, closing in from 250 yards to 100 yards. My No 2, Sgt Ross, then came in to attack. I saw two members of the crew bail out. A few seconds later the aircraft hit the ground and was burnt out.'

A week later 'Jumbo' Genders scrambled again, and an extract from one of his letters vividly described the sortie's dramatic events;

'Early in September (6th) it was reported that another Ju 86 was coming in from over the sea. Plt Off Gold and I took off together. We sighted the aircraft about 50 miles east of Alexandria, and the Germans

Canadian 'Red' Chisholm achieved all of his six and two shared victories over the desert during 1942-43, mostly flying Spitfires with No 92 Sqn. He claimed his fifth victory on 1 September 1942 (*via C F Shores*)

Sgt 'Sammy' Samouelle of No 92 Sqn used BR523/QJ-E to shoot down a Bf 109 for his second victory and also claimed another Messerschmitt as a 'probable' on 19 August 1942. He then had to force land alongside the main Alexandria-Mersa Matruh road, however (*ww2images*)

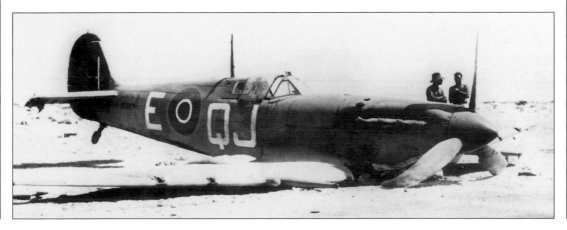

must have sighted us at the same time as the aircraft began to fly back again over the sea. I caught up to it when about 100 miles from land, and with my two machine guns (the others had been taken out to lighten the aircraft) I stopped one of the Junkers' engines – saw hits on the fuselage and starboard engine. I now turned back, as I had only about three gallons of petrol left.

'Gold, who with his heavier Spitfire was several thousand feet below, waited until the Junkers lost height and then gave it the coup de grace. Gold got back to the airfield with a few gallons of petrol to spare, but I ran out of petrol when still a long way from the coast. The land was out of sight when I bailed out at the minimum safe height, but I swam south, guiding myself by the sun and reached land on a deserted stretch of the Egyptian coast.'

Genders, in an incredible feat of endurance, had swum for 21 hours and eventually returned to Aboukir, having effectively ended these high altitude intrusions, for the German unit undertaking them had only three Ju 86Ps on strength. The loss of two of them in such a short period all but curtailed their activities.

VICTORY AT ALAMEIN

Back in the Western Desert, at dusk on 30 August Rommel began his move against the Alamein line and the Battle of Alam Halfa commenced, so presaging heavy fighting. The German push to reach the Nile Delta and to cut the Suez Canal was soon halted, and within a few days the enemy had withdrawn to his own defensive line following a counter attack on 3 September. The Alam Halfa assault was the enemy's last offensive in North Africa, for the relentless Allied build up that had now started would continue until the decisive battle of El Alamein some six weeks later.

Intense aerial operations were flown throughout this period, and on the opening day of the enemy offensive No 92 Sqn's Sqn Ldr Jeff Wedgewood achieved acedom while providing top cover to a sweep near El Daba when he shot down a 4° *Stormo* C.202. No 601 Sqn's youthful Bruce Ingram gained a further distinction a week later when, on 7 September, he shot down a Bf 109 of I./JG 27 to become the first pilot to claim five Spitfire victories in the desert campaign.

'Hoodless' Spitfire VB BR476/QJ-J was the favoured mount of the CO of No 92 Sqn, Sqn Ldr Jeff Wedgewood. In it he claimed six of his victories, including two Bf 109s during the 'weather blitz' of 9 October 1942 (*S M Coates*)

Seen after being commissioned, Londoner 'Sammy' Samouelle became an ace in the heavy fighting that preceded the Battle of El Alamein (*ww2images*)

A few days later No 145 Sqn's new CO, Sqn Ldr Peter Matthews, also became an ace when, having been scrambled after a Stuka raid, he shot down one of the escorting fighters. However, on the 16th his squadron suffered a sad loss. At 0950 hrs eight Spitfires scrambled with No 601 Sqn as top cover to Kittyhawks chasing a Stuka formation over the Alamein line, and Flt Lt Joseph Sabourin shot down one of the escorting Bf 109s for his seventh victory. However, at 1700 hrs during another scramble he was hit by the *experte* Unteroffizier von Arnoldy of III./JG 27 and his Spitfire blew up, killing the WDAF's first Spitfire ace, as the squadron diarist soberly recorded;

'They saw 12+ ME 109s and MC 202s. Flt Lt Sabourin destroyed a 109. Three other enemy aircraft were damaged. Flt Lt Sabourin was shot down. His aircraft exploded on striking the ground and he was killed.'

The preparations for the coming Battle of El Alamein included attrition of the enemy's air capability. A period of bad weather flooded Axis airfields around El Daba, and on 9 October the WDAF conducted a 'weather blitz' on the enemy airfields in the area. While escorting fighter-bombers, No 92 Sqn, led by Sqn Ldr Wedgewood, engaged five Bf 109s at 12,000 ft, three of which were shot down. Two fell to the CO and the other was claimed by Plt Off 'Sammy' Samouelle, who became an ace. Also continuing his path to acedom was 20-year-old Flg Off 'Babe' Whitamore of No 601 Sqn, who was credited with a Bf 109 too.

The WDAF maintained the increasing pressure on the enemy frontline through October, flying fighter patrols over enemy airfields which in turn ensured that Allied attack aircraft had an increased freedom of movement. For example, on 23 October – the day before the Allied offensive commenced – from 0700 hrs No 145 Sqn flew three missions to cover Kittyhawks. Nine more took off at midday for an offensive sweep to Daba, near where they met enemy aircraft, as the Operational Record Book described;

'Sqn Ldr Matthews attacked an ME 109F at 800 yards, and the enemy aircraft rolled over and fell away with a long streamer of smoke coming out. The aircraft fell vertically for 11,000 ft and has been confirmed as destroyed. Flt Sgt Powers saw two ME 109s flying west. He attacked the rear one from astern and the aircraft gave out black smoke, changing to white, and went down in a dive. An aircraft was seen burning at the point the enemy aircraft would have fallen, and Flt Sgt Powers was given a destroyed for this combat. Plt Off Small confirms.'

It was Peter Matthews' seventh victory, whilst for 'Mac' Powers, an American in the RAF, it was the start of his path to acedom.

Further back, the No 103 MU flight, now led by successful ace Flt Lt Mike Cooper-Slipper, also continued to see some action, as on 21 October. He recalled fellow ace Eric Genders as 'A very quiet, very brave officer, who claimed his tenth victory when he shot down a Ju 88 on a reconnaissance near Heliopolis, although was flying a standard Spitfire VB. He chased it through cloud, firing from line astern, seeing his fire striking the wing adjacent to the engines and causing one of them to fail. The aircraft came down in German lines.'

The decisive Battle of El Alamein opened on a narrow front with a massive artillery barrage during the evening of 23 October, and the three Spitfire units were out early the following morning covering fighter bombers and countering enemy air attacks as Axis forces fiercely resisted the 'push'.

In succeeding days the RAF was committed to preventing any attempt at the enemy concentrating its forces and in interdicting the Axis supply lines, so there were innumerable combats fought. For example, during the afternoon of the 25th over the central sector of the front a quartet of Spitfires from No 92 Sqn attacked two Bf 109s, one of which was shot down into the sea by Flt Lt John Morgan for

his sixth victory. A short while later five more Bf 109s were attacked by a patrol from No 145 Sqn, allowing Flt Lt Cecil Saunders to claim his seventh, and last, success.

In spite of the efforts of the WDAF Allied armour was unable to break the enemy's defensive positions, and the fighting on, and over, the front continued unabated, especially around Kidney Ridge where the Allies suffered heavy losses. It was during the continued action over this area on 27 October that Australian Kittyhawk ace Flg Off John Waddy of No 92 Sqn claimed his second Spitfire kill when he destroyed a Bf 109. He claimed another three days later to take his final tally to an impressive 15.5 victories. The action around Kidney Ridge intensified as the battle approached its climax, with Allied air power becoming increasingly more influential as it prevented the enemy from rapidly marshalling its armoured forces. In the air losses on both sides were considerable.

On 2 November Gen Sir Bernard Montgomery instigated Operation *Supercharge* and the New Zealand Division at last broke through Axis lines. Despite frantic enemy resistance, other units managed to force a way through to the south of Kidney Ridge. Overhead, air combat continued, and during a morning patrol No 601 Sqn's Spitfires were successful. Among those claiming kills was Plt Off Desmond Ibbotson, while later in the day No 92 Sqn's 'Sammy' Samouelle bagged a Bf 109. By that evening Rommel had decided to withdraw, but Axis forces doggedly resisted nevertheless.

On 3 November, during the day's first operation, No 145 Sqn's CO, Sqn Ldr Peter Matthews, ditched just off the coast but was safely picked up, as unit records describe;

'Nine aircraft were ordered to climb to 25,000 ft, at which point six '109s were seen to pass directly overhead. Fifteen '109s were met at the same height as ourselves, and 15+ Stukas were observed at 15,000 ft dead below. Sqn Ldr Matthews said "Okay, going down", and White Section dived into the '109s and the top section turned about as further '109s came down. Sqn Ldr Matthews was shot down into the sea (subsequently rescued unhurt) and Plt Off Duigan did not return.'

Finally, on 4 November after further heavy fighting, the 8th Army began a general breakout and the race across the desert after the *Afrika Corps* began. Above, a patrol of No 145 Sqn's Spitfires over El Daba shot

One of the leading RAAF pilots of World War 2, Flt Lt John Waddy sits on the rear fuselage of a captured Bf 109F of JG 27 in late 1942. He claimed the last three of his 15.5 victories in Spitfires with No 92 Sqn. His remaining kills came flying Tomahawks and Kittyhawks in North Africa, both with the RAF and the SAAF. Waddy later commanded an RAAF Kittyhawk squadron in the Pacific (*via John Weal*)

Sqn Ldr Jeff Wedgewood poses for the camera in his aircraft on a desert strip at the time of the Battle of El Alamein. The fighter is marked with all of his victories to that date, including those from the Battle of Britain. Tragically, Wedgewood was killed shortly afterwards whilst en route back to England (*No 92 Sqn Records*)

Seen at the start of his tour with No 92 Sqn, Flg Off Neville Duke had his then extant score of eight victories recorded on the cockpit of his aircraft (ER220/QJ-R), and to which he soon added further symbols. The 20-year-old was to become the most successful Allied fighter pilot in the Mediterranean (*N F Duke*)

down three Bf 109s, including one each to future aces Plt Off Alastair Wilson and Flt Sgt 'Mac' Powers.

Enemy harassment and extensive minefields slowed the Allied advance, while heavy rain bogged down both armour and air support, allowing Axis forces a significant head start in their retreat. The speed of the withdrawal was breathtaking, and the race for Benghazi began. Spitfire squadrons regularly moved forward during this period, taking off from Egyptian airfields and then returning to newly captured landing grounds in Libya. The enemy's problems were exacerbated by the Anglo-American *Torch* landings in French North Africa on 7 November, which opened a new front that in turn needed to be countered with scarce resources, thus indirectly helping the push west from Egypt.

Additional Spitfire deliveries also allowed re-equipment of a further unit, and No 1 Sqn SAAF at LG 173 duly received its first four machines on 4 November. When it returned to operations ten days later it also had a new CO in the form of Maj Peter Metelerkamp. At the same time Sqn Ldr Jeff Wedgewood, who had led No 92 Sqn with such distinction whilst personally claiming nine destroyed, handed over to Sqn Ldr John Morgan, who had aces Flt Lts 'Sammy' Samouelle and 'Red' Chisholm as his flight commanders. The unit also welcomed a notable new arrival too when Flg Off Neville Duke re-joined, flying his first sortie on 19 November – the day British troops entered Benghazi. He noted in his diary 'I always fly with the hood back now – am getting to like it and can see lots more. Must not get jumped this time!'

Indeed, No 92 Sqn removed the hoods from all of its aircraft for a brief period, but later re-fitted them. The Spitfires were also stripped of extraneous equipment in expectation of the unit meeting the Fw 190s that were anticipated in-theatre at any moment.

No 145 Sqn also gained an experienced ace CO when Sqn Ldr Roy Marples arrived on the 22nd – he was described as a 'very young, bouncy, effervescent man'. Soon after the unit settled in M'sus, deep into Cyrenaica, alongside the other Spitfire squadrons in-theatre. It was from there on the 27th that No 1 Sqn SAAF had its first combat since receiving Spitfires when, at 0730 hrs, the CO led his unit into combat against a group of Bf 109s near Mersa-el-Brega, one of which he damaged. Later that same day at about 1530 hrs, Peter Metelerkamp shot down a Bf 109 in flames to claim his fifth victory. Also achieving acedom in the same combat was Capt Johannes Faure, whose victim crash-landed. Future ace Lt Harry Gaynor damaged two more, but these successes came at the cost of two Spitfires.

From M'sus the Spitfires flew sweeps into Tripolitania, and when No 601 Sqn performed such a mission on 5 December the unit spotted a formation of Bf 109s near Marble Arch at 16,000 ft. In the brief action which ensued Plt Off Desmond Ibbotson shot one of the German

fighters down. However, when gaining his seventh victory two days later he had to force land himself and was captured by some of Rommel's staff. He was presented to the 'Desert Fox' himself, but that night escaped and, with the help of some friendly Arabs, Ibbotson returned with his remarkable story!

Conducting 'delousing' missions for fighter-bomber aircraft was a primary task for the Spitfire squadrons, as they were equipped with the highest performance fighters available to the RAF in the desert. It was during one such sortie that No 601 Sqn's Flt Lt Bruce Ingram claimed his ninth, and last, victory in North Africa. In the Mersa-el-Brega area he bounced a solitary Bf 109 that was attacking his Kittyhawk charges, sending I./JG 77's Feldwebel Hacker down in flames. The other Spitfire units were also successful over the next few days, but No 1 Sqn SAAF suffered a severe loss on the 13th when Peter Metelerkamp's brief glory ended during an attack on a Ju 88. Hit by return fire, his engine streamed glycol and he crashed to his death to the north of Benghazi. He was replaced later in the month by another future ace, Sqn Ldr Peter Olver.

The squadrons were highly mobile and continued to leapfrog forward regularly, usually to strips that were in reality flat areas of desert that had been crudely marked out. M'sus, for example, was described by Flg Off Bert Houle (a future ace who joined No 145 Sqn there) as 'a small rocky aerodrome on a ridge with a very narrow runway that was marked off with stones that had been removed while making it'. Of his introduction to the Spitfire, Houle said;

'It was love from the start, although I made the common mistake of over-controlling on take-off and floating too far when coming in to land. This ship was superb in the air and seemed reluctant to settle down when landing. After having a go at aerobatics and spinning, a practice dogfight and a test of the guns on a ground target, I was ready for operations!'

Houle had his first action in the Spitfire on 7 December when covering No 92 Sqn. 'I ended up with two to myself and got in a two-second burst. I should have done some damage but didn't'.

Soon afterwards, the 8th Army began its assault on the El Agheila line. By the turn of the year the four Spitfire units had moved to, or were

On 4 December 1942 Spitfire VC EP690/AX-A of No 1 Sqn SAAF, flown by Lt Doug Rogan (who had three victories, two probables and three damaged to his name), collided with EP245 at El Hassiat. AX-A was the usual mount of the CO, Maj Peter Metelerkamp, who on 27 November had used it to shoot down a Bf 109 for his fifth victory. EP690 was repaired and subsequently issued to No 40 Sqn SAAF, only to be shot down over Sicily on 10 July 1943, killing Capt G C le Roux (*S M Coates*)

soon to arrive at, the desert strip at Alem El Chel, some 30 miles south east of Sirte and deep into Libyan territory.

Further back in the Nile Delta area No 417 Sqn – the only RCAF fighter squadron in the Mediterranean – had gradually been re-equipped with Spitfires. It was initially held back at Idku for the defence of Alexandria, with detachments at Heliopolis, outside Cairo, and in the oasis at Kufra, deep in the desert. In addition, the No 103 MU Spitfire element had moved to El Gamil, near Port Said, where it was parented by the resident No 94 Sqn. The four Spitfire VBs were there to handle any high altitude interceptions, while No 94 Sqn's Hurricane IIs worked lower down. The Spitfire detachment was led by Flt Lt Richard Webb, while No 94 Sqn included Rhodesian ace Plt Off Eric Dicks-Sherwood among its number.

Throughout December this flight carried out scrambles and patrols to counter high-flying reconnaissance aircraft. The highlight came late on the morning of 20 December when Webb and Flg Off Rowland caught and shot down a Ju 88 of 2.(F)/123. They had been scrambled to the northwest, and after their attack saw three parachutes and the intruder crash into the sea. This was the second of Webb's four victories, and the last by a Spitfire over Egypt and Libya in 1942. During its first sixth months in North Africa the Spitfire VB had successfully challenged the Bf 109F for the mastery of the skies in-theatre.

THE MARETH LINE

As 1943 opened it was evident that the Luftwaffe was far from beaten, and in the early days of January Bf 109s flew several successful strafing attacks on landing grounds around Hamraiet. On the 7th, for the first time since El Alamein, No 92 Sqn met enemy fighters in large numbers that stayed and fought, and two Bf 109s from II./JG 77 were destroyed. Climbing to 12,000 ft, John Morgan claimed his eighth, and last, success. The other victory went to former US 'Eagle' squadron pilot Flg Off Leo Nomis, but two Spitfires were also lost, the diarist noting, 'These are not the demoralised pilots who moved out of Daba in November'.

Strafing attacks by Bf 109s and C.202s were repeated the next day, the first raid being intercepted at 0815 hrs by No 145 Sqn and resulting in Flt Lt Bert Houle shooting a Messerschmitt down. It was the Canadian's first victory in a Spitfire, but it elevated him to ace status;

'I got behind one which flew straight into the sun and fired a few bursts at him. The pilot panicked and turned down sun while diving for ground level. When he levelled out I was a few thousand feet above him, and I used my height to close the gap between us. When well within range, I pressed the firing button and two cannons and four machine guns started to register hits. I knocked the radiator and large pieces of the fuselage off and was closing in for the finish when there was a clattering and banging beneath my aircraft. I thought there must be a '109 on my tail and broke sharply to starboard. There was nothing there, but I discovered later that some New Zealand gunners had been shooting at the '109 and had shot with too little deflection. My aircraft had run into their fire. I eased back on the power and limped for our forward base.

'Shortly after landing, Wingco Darwen called me to explain that the New Zealanders had picked up the German pilot, who had asked

Now with a dozen victories recorded, No 92 Sqn's ER220 suffered the indignity of nosing over on a rough Libyan strip in early 1943. The fighter was Neville Duke's regular mount between November 1942 and February 1943, and in it he shot down a C.202 on 8 January and a pair of Ju 87s 13 days later (*ww2images*)

John Taylor, seen here as a flight lieutenant with No 145 Sqn at about the time of the Battle of El Alamein, claimed all of his 15 victories flying Spitfires with Nos 145 and 601 Sqns over North Africa and Sicily. He became an ace in January 1943. Tragically, after scoring his last success on 12 July 1943 over Sicily, the 23-year-old CO of No 601 Sqn was hit by return fire and died in the subsequent crash (*via N L R Franks*)

to meet his adversary. He was a tall, slim, alert looking lad in his early twenties.'

Houle's victim was Feldwebel Friedal Behrend of 3./JG 77 who had been flying new Bf 109G-2, Wk-Nr 10575 'Yellow 3'.

Two hours later it was No 92 Sqn's Spitfires that intercepted the next raid, as Flg Off Neville Duke wrote in his diary;

'Scrambled in the morning and came across Stukas and '109s bombing our forward troops. Got stuck in to the top cover of Macchi 202s at 13,000 ft. The boys had a pretty hard fight as the Macchis stayed and fought. I dived on two slightly below, with Flt Sgt Sales. We were well placed and in the sun – they never saw us until it was too late when they put their noses down for home, but we were on them. The one I chased went down vertically from 10,000 ft to the deck and drew smoke from him with a cannon shell in his radiator and oil cooler. He finally hit the ground and burst into flames after some more hits from my cannons which were working well this day! The aircraft dissolved into flame and small pieces. Quite a scrap.'

Duke's ninth victory was the first of his new tour, while his wingman claimed another. Both Nos 601 and 1 SAAF Sqns were also engaged during the day. The Spitfire units were in action again over the next few days, particularly on the 11th when No 92 Sqn's Neville Duke gave himself a 21st birthday present in the form of a brace of C.202s that he found near Tamit. He fired on the first and saw strikes near the cockpit;

'He rolled over and I had a glimpse of the pilot pulling himself out of the cockpit. Saw his 'chute open nicely and his machine go down – pieces still coming off. Confirmed by rest of the squadron. This pilot was taken prisoner. He was the CO of a fighter group – some catch!'

In a confused dogfight as the formation broke up Duke had another opportunity and sent a second Macchi down, this time to a crash landing;

'He was out of his cockpit before the dust had settled. I sympathised with him, having had the same experience. I gave him a wave!'

His victims were Maggiore Gustavo Garretto and Sottotenente Tellerchi from 18° *Gruppo*, who both became prisoners.

The Italians were in action over Tamet again on 12 January when No 1 Sqn SAAF provided top cover to No 145 Sqn, whose CO, Sqn Ldr Roy Marples, achieved his final victory when he attacked a C.200 of 13° *Gruppo* at low level and saw strikes with his first burst, followed by black smoke. His second burst sent the Macchi into the sea just off the coast. However, Marples' fighter too suffered an engine failure and he was forced to ditch just offshore. Fortunately his predicament was seen and two soldiers swam out to rescue him.

Sgt Dennis Usher was also successful that day, claiming his first success on the Spitfire when, after chasing the Macchis, he was overtaken by a Bf 109 attacking another No 145 Sqn machine. Switching targets, he got onto the Messerschmitt's tail and hit it in both wings, causing the fighter to pull up. Usher followed, still firing, until the Bf 109 shuddered into a stall and went down vertically. Also successful was Flt Lt John Taylor who 'made ace' when he downed a C.200 in the same action.

These heavy skirmishes in the Tamet area continued over succeeding days as an offensive to clear the latest enemy defensive line at Buerat commenced, the Spitfires continuing to 'delouse' fighter-bombers. One such mission took place on the 14th when No 1 Sqn SAAF covered USAAF P-40s south of Buerat. Lt 'Robbie' Robinson, a future ace, shot down a Bf 109F (probably 'Black 11' of I./JG 77, flown by Unteroffizier Hans Jakobi) that ventured too close to the Warhawks. Also returning to action with No 601 Sqn that day following a rest was New Zealand ace Flt Lt Derek Westenra, who made his first Spitfire claim when he damaged a Bf 109.

On 16 January Rommel issued the order to pull back, and as his forces headed for the Tunisian border they were constantly harassed by the WDAF and advanced elements of the pursuing 8th Army. Homs, only 60 miles east of Tripoli, fell to the 51st Highland Division on 19 January, resulting in a further move forward for supporting squadrons – all four Spitfire units occupied Wadi Surri (Darragh North), for example.

Covering the push towards Tripoli during the morning of 21 January, a patrol of No 1 Sqn SAAF Spitfires was forced to descend because of cloud cover. Once nearer the ground the ten Spitfires spotted a trio of C.202s near Castel Verde. Peter Olver's section quickly turned left and climbed into the attack, resulting in both he and Capt Harry Gaynor destroying one each and Lt Doug Rogan probably destroying the third. This was a real tonic for No 1 Sqn SAAF, which had undergone an unhappy time since the loss of its previous CO. Several hours later the No 244 Wing Leader, Wg Cdr Johnny Darwen, led a daylight sweep over Tripoli by No 92 Sqn and intercepted a formation of Ju 87s that had been spotted by Neville Duke. The latter promptly dived on them, scoring a few hits on one before turning his attention to a second;

'Attacked second one and closed, fired and hit him in starboard wing root, which burst into flames. Ju 87 went down in spirals and exploded on hitting the ground. My 12th victory.'

Two others were credited to 'Sammy' Samouelle and Flg Off Milt Jowsey also destroyed one to embark on his path to acedom. It was a successful final sortie for Samouelle, whose position as OC 'A' Flight was taken by Duke following promotion to flight lieutenant.

On 22 January the last German troops evacuated Tripoli, which was occupied by the Allies the following day. This in turn led to a curtailment in operations by the WDAF. Its units prepared to move

Two Ju 87s of III./StG 3 are captured by Neville Duke's camera gun as he closes astern in an engagement near Castel Benito on 21 January 1943. He duly shot two of the dive-bombers down (*N F Duke via N L R Franks*)

Spitfire VC ER228/ZX-S of No 145 Sqn was used by Flt Lt John Taylor to claim his eighth victory (a C.202) during the fighting over the Mareth Line, in Tunisia, on 7 March 1943 (*via R C Sturtivant*)

Spitfire VC ES252/ZX-E of No 145 Sqn powers up on its take-off roll on a desert strip with unit CO, and ace, Sqn Ldr Lance Wade at its controls. His regular aircraft throughout the spring of 1943, the American made three claims in it during March, including a Bf 109 destroyed on the 22nd – his 16th kill overall and second in the Spitfire (*ww2images*)

into the more permanent facilities at Castel Benito to prepare for future operations against the new and well prepared enemy defensive position – the formidable Mareth Line. The end of January also saw No 145 Sqn welcome a new CO when Sqn Ldr Lance Wade took over. Nicknamed 'Wildcat', the American had an impressive record from his previous time on Hurricanes, having accumulated 14 victories. Also flying with No 145 before taking up his post as leader of No 244 Wing in February was another ace, Wg Cdr 'Widge' Gleed. His arrival coincided with the wing being further reinforced by the arrival of the now fully equipped No 417 Sqn at Castel Benito.

The Mareth Line was a system of fortifications built by the French in southern Tunisia before the war against any possible attack from the Italians in Libya, and it covered the only easy approach to the settled areas in the north of the country. The wadi on which the Line was based was a natural defensive position, with steep 70 ft high banks that made it virtually impregnable.

Shaping operations soon began, with the occupation of Medenine and Ben Gardane in mid February resulting in further aerial engagments

as the enemy countered Allied air attacks. Typical was the dogfight No 145 Sqn had when scrambled on 26 February, four aircraft chasing two Bf 109s that were caught over Bordj Touaz. John Taylor fired several bursts at one, causing the fighter's starboard wing to crumple before it exploded. He hit the second one before running out of ammunition.

The enemy was by no means finished, and Hazdub, to where No 244 Wing had moved, came under heavy shellfire on 1 March, forcing a rapid and rather undignified exit back to Ben Gardane. That same day John Taylor downed a Bf 109, his victim bailing out, while his CO, Sqn Ldr Lance Wade, claimed his first victory with the squadron. No 92 Sqn was also engaged, Neville Duke downing two C.202s. He was to claim four more kills over the next week alone. The wing received a significant reinforcement on 11 March with the arrival of 17 experienced Polish pilots attached to No 145 Sqn as the 'Polish Fighting Team' (PFT), and they would be led in the air by their leading ace, Sqn Ldr Stanislaw Skalski.

On the ground preparations continued for the attack, aerial reconnaissance confirming that the Mareth Line could be outflanked through the Tebaga Gap from its western end. The classic 'left hook' manoeuvre was entrusted to Lt Gen Bernard Freyberg's New Zealand Corps. They advanced on the night of 19 March to move on El Hamma, and thus outflank the Line, and the following night the main body of the 8th Army began the frontal assault. They were directly supported by WDAF fighter-bombers, covered by Spitfires of No 244 Wing. On the 20th No 1 Sqn SAAF scrambled after a radar 'plot' and engaged a mixed formation of enemy fighters to the southwest of Medenine. As the enemy aircraft broke up, Lt J R Lanham fired at an Fw 190 from close range and sent it spinning into the desert – this is thought to have been the first Focke-Wulf destroyed in the desert.

No 417 Sqn opened its Spitfire account on 22 March when four fighters downed an He 111 torpedo-bomber off the coast.

No 244 Wing accepted delivery of 12 Spitfire IXs on the 23rd – a welcome sight following the arrival of Fw 190s. Six were issued to No 145 Sqn's PFT and four to No 92 Sqn, as Neville Duke noted;

'We operated a mixed formation of Mk Vs and IXs, with the Vs leading (because of their lower performance) and the IXs flying as high top cover and ranging freely at higher speed. If I remember correctly, we used to patrol in the IXs at medium altitude at about 240 mph indicated air speed.'

On 24 March Allied bombers targeted enemy forces holding back the New Zealanders battling through the Tebaga Gap, and among those engaged near El Hamma was Rhodesian Flt Lt Ian Shand of No 145 Sqn, who

The arrival of the Fw 190 in the skies over North Africa had been anticipated for some time, and they began to be encountered over Tunisia in the early spring of 1943. The first one shot down in-theatre fell to the guns of this aircraft, Spitfire VC ER882/AX-F of No 1 Sqn SAAF, flown by Lt J R Lanham on 20 March. Sadly, Lanham was subsequently killed in it when he crashed whilst trying to land at Sfax in late May (SAAF)

attacked a Bf 109 and saw explosions in the starboard wing, followed by a flash on the ground for his second confirmed victory.

Attacks on the enemy around El Hamma continued unabated on 25 March, and No 1 Sqn SAAF was heavily tasked, flying a bomber escort in the morning. Then at 1500 hrs a scramble was ordered, during which Lt 'Robbie' Robinson attacked an 'Me 210' that crashed and burned. A late afternoon patrol by the unit became embroiled with around 20 enemy fighters, and Lt van Nus destroyed a Bf 109 near El Hamma while Lts Brebner and van de Merwe got a C.202 each between Gabes and El Hamma. However, Lt Tyrell was killed, while the unfortunate Lt H F Smith collided with a C.202 and crashed to his death.

The line finally cracked the next day, and on 27 March, as British armour poured through the Tebaga Gap, the Mareth Line was effectively turned and only desperate fighting allowed the enemy to escape. The air fighting over El Hamma remained intense, and just before midday six Spitfires from No 145 Sqn scrambled and spotted ten Ju 88s, probably from III./KG 77 at 10,000 ft. The Spitfires, which were some 4000 ft higher, dived on the bombers and forced them to jettison their loads. Five stragglers were then caught, Plt Off Dennis Usher achieving acedom when the aircraft he was chasing went into a spiral dive and crashed into the ground. The next day the PFT drew its first blood when a flight led by Skalski engaged a group of Ju 88s and their Bf 109 escorts. After a short fight, Skalski and Flt Lt Eugeniusz Horbaczewski each downed a bomber.

The main defensive line in the south was broken and the road to Tunis, and the link up with the *Torch* forces, had been opened.

In early 1943 Hurricane II-equipped No 33 Sqn at Bersis received four Spitfire VBs, two of which are seen here after delivery. The middle aircraft was air tested by the unit CO, nine-victory ace Sqn Ldr Stan Norris, on 2 February and flown on several other occasions until he left later in the month. No 33 Sqn's only Spitfire victory in Egypt was claimed on 1 May 1943 when Flt Lt Sandy Kallio brought down a Ju 88 during a convoy escort (*M Naydler*)

TORCH TO TUNIS

While the 8th Army had been preparing for its El Alamein offensive, in Britain a large operation was set in motion that would see Anglo-American forces inserted in the Vichy French-controlled colonies of Morocco and Algeria with the intention of hitting Rommel's forces from the rear. The British bastion of Gibraltar played a key part in the November 1942 invasion, not least as the location for the assembly of land-based fighters that were then flown from there to newly-captured airfields in Algeria. Amongst the units despatched were a large number of Spitfire V squadrons, although the Supermarine fighter had seen action over the Western Mediterranean prior to the Operation *Torch* landings actually taking place.

At Gibraltar was a small unit known as 'Y' Squadron or 'Gib Flight' which was charged with providing the air defence of the colony, and among its pilots was New Zealander Flg Off H A 'Joe' Crafts. On 11 October he was scrambled in Spitfire VC EP444 after an unknown 'plot'. Vectored onto reconnaissance Ju 88D 'F6+KK', Crafts succeeded in forcing it to crash-land near Melilla, in Spanish Morocco.

During the early hours of 8 November, a little over two weeks after the opening of the Alamein offensive, Operation *Torch* saw the landing of forces near the Algerian cities of Algiers and Oran, and at Casablanca, in Morocco. Initial air cover for the invasion was provided by carrier-based fighters. At Algiers all went well, with no serious resistance being encountered from the Vichy French forces. Indeed, at 0830 hrs units in Gibraltar were told, somewhat prematurely, that the vital airfield at Maison Blanche was in Allied hands. By that stage a Hurricane squadron was already inbound, and it landed soon afterwards, followed two hours later by the Spitfires of Nos 81 and 242 Sqns. The latter were led by No 322 Wing Leader and Battle of Britain ace Wg Cdr P H 'Dutch' Hugo. He would soon significantly increase his score. Among his pilots was a future ace with No 81 Sqn, 20-year-old New Zealander Sgt Alan Peart, who recalled the almost farcical situation they found upon their arrival;

'Despite earlier reports to the contrary, the airfield at Maison Blanche was still under the control of the Vichy French forces, and one of our Spitfire Vs was shot down by a Dewoitine 520 fighter as it landed. An argument ensued between Sqn Ldr "Ras" Berry and the French base commander as to who was who's prisoner! Fortunately, a British tank appeared on the scene, and it was clear that the airfield would be taken.'

Although Vichy-French resistance continued at Oran and Casablanca for several days, by the 9th Algiers was firmly under Allied control. Characteristically, the Germans, although completely surprised, reacted swiftly and decisively so that 24 hours after the landings they were pouring aircraft and troops into El Aouina, near Tunis. More than 100 aircraft had been seen there on the 10th, while transport aircraft were arriving at nearby Bizerte at a rate of 50 a day.

Air action for the Spitfire units was thus not long in coming as on 9 November two fighters shot down a Ju 88 on a reconnaissance mission.

Patrols continued over the Allied shipping off Algiers, and later in the afternoon just as dusk was falling a large raid of unescorted bombers appeared. Both the Spitfires of No 81 Sqn and a number of Hurricanes were scrambled, and they were joined by 13 fighters from No 242 Sqn that were already airborne to escort the two B-17s carrying US Army Gen

Mark Clark and his staff in from Gibraltar. A terrific battle ensued in which several of No 242 Sqn's pilots opened their accounts over North Africa, as the unit records described;

'The squadron started its first day well as follows – Sgt Mallinson shot down an He 111 into the sea in flames, Plt Off Goulding and Sgt Watling destroyed a Ju 88 apiece and Flt Lt Benham and Plt Off Mather shared a Ju 88 destroyed during their dusk patrol. Plt Offs Portz and Lamberd, Sqn Ldr Secretan and Plt Off Lindsay got a half-kill each, and they all damaged a Ju 88, as did Plt Off Hampshire. This took place when Ju 88s were bombing a convoy off Algiers. There were three waves of Ju 88s and He 111s, and the units at Maison Blanche destroyed 12.'

Not to be outdone, No 81 Sqn's CO, Sqn Ldr 'Ras' Berry, and his section attacked an He 111 over the airfield at low-level, riddling the Heinkel and forcing it down two miles from Maison Blanche. Also successful was Canadian Flt Lt James Walker, who already had two victories to his name from service in Russia and the UK. He shot down a Ju 88 to start a great run of success over the next few months. For the fighter pilots involved, the only thing that bettered this success was the delivery of the first food to North Africa since their arrival!

From Algiers British troops pushed eastwards towards Tunisia with all despatch. 'Dutch' Hugo and Flt Lt 'Shag' Eckford of No 154 Sqn brought down an obsolescent Do 17 (probably a 'hack' used by JG 53) near Bougie on the 12th. The very next day, as Allied troops neared Bougie itself, Eckford destroyed a Ju 88 and shared in the destruction of another. By then No 111 Sqn had arrived from Gibraltar and No 324 Wing (with Nos 72 and 152 Sqns) had set up at Maison Blanche, where it was joined by No 93 Sqn – the latter unit soon moved east to Souk el Arba, however. The 13th also saw No 154 Sqn's Kiwi CO, Sqn Ldr Don Carlson (with two and two shared victories to his name from his time with No 74 Sqn in 1941), shoot down a Ju 88 off Algeria to become the first Spitfire pilot to reach acedom over French North Africa.

Carlson's pilots approached the new theatre with zeal and confidence, and in their first fortnight of operations they claimed 19 enemy bombers destroyed, three more probably destroyed and six damaged. The enemy vigorously contested the skies, however. On 14 November Flg Off Harry Fenwick, a Canadian in No 81 Sqn, fell victim to a Bf 109 of JG 53 and had to force land with a minor leg wound. Two days later, near Bougie, he damaged a Bf 109, although his own Spitfire was again damaged by a Bf 109 from II./JG 53. Fenwick got his revenge the next day when he shot down a C.202 – the first of his six victories. He bagged a Bf 109 the following day too.

Wearing the short lived single letter unit codes used at the time of Operation *Torch*, No 242 Sqn's Spitfire VC ER676/B-E is seen after a minor mishap. Flt Lt Douglas Benham was flying this machine on 4 December 1942 when he probably destroyed an Fw 190 near Mateur (*D I Benham*)

The RAF's only Icelandic pilot, Flt Sgt 'Tony' Jonsson claimed four kills over Algeria and Tunisia with No 111 Sqn and became an ace in 1944 when flying Mustang IIIs with No 65 Sqn (*via C F Shores*)

Sitting at Souk el Khemis in early 1943, No 93 Sqn's *Yellow Peril* (Spitfire VC ER979/J-J) was occasionally flown by Sgt Francis Campbell, the first time on 16 January. However, from 19 February it became the usual mount of Sgt John Humphrey, who used it on 5 April to damage a Bf 109 and probably destroy an Fw 190 the following day. Sadly, on the 17th he was shot down in an air battle off Cap Serron and killed (*Peter Arnold Collection*)

After several abortive scrambles, soon after dawn on the 15th success came No 111 Sqn's way when the RAF's only Icelandic fighter pilot, Flt Sgt T E 'Tony' Jonsson, claimed his first victory;

'At first light I led a section of four aircraft on a patrol line between the harbour and the aerodrome. I caught sight of a formation of six bombers nearing the harbour, flying at about 3000 ft just below the clouds. We immediately turned towards them, and as we got closer we could see that they were He 111 bombers. I switched on my reflector sight, thumbed off the safety catch for the guns, pressed the R/T button and announced as calmly as I could "Okay lads, now's our chance. I'll go for the leader and each one picks his own target. Let's clobber the lot!"

'When the bomber crews saw us approaching they seemed to panic and the formation broke up. The adversary I had chosen was already in a tight climbing turn heading for the clouds, and just before he disappeared I sent him a long burst from my cannons at maximum range. I saw no signs of having hit him, and once again I had reason to curse my poor marksmanship. But this time I was determined not to let him escape. The clouds were ragged and not too large, and I was bound to find him again. Oh yes, there he was, slightly out to the right. But before I got within range he disappeared into cloud. I ground my teeth and cursed some more. Hell, this one simply must not get away!

'The pilot of the Heinkel was cunning and continually changed course in the clouds so that each time he emerged again he was out of range. At last after about ten minutes of this grotesque game of hide and seek, I guessed right. We came out of cloud flying line abreast about 100 yards apart, and by making a sharp right turn I was able to get in a burst of machine gun and cannon fire. Even I could not miss at this short range, and just before we entered cloud again I observed bright flashes near the wing root. Now I was bound to get him. My heart was beating a tattoo and I had a feeling of euphoria.

'A few seconds later we both came out of cloud. The German had turned to starboard and I now found myself slightly above and behind him – he was a sitting duck. I saw tracer bullets curving towards me from the Heinkel's gun turret but this I ignored, and from very close range I sent him a long burst of fire and saw the right hand engine explode. I had to take fast evasive action to avoid flying into debris from it, and once again we were both engulfed in cloud. About 30 seconds later I emerged from cloud. A short time later I caught sight of a column of smoke and then a great splash on the surface of the sea a short distance off the coast. I felt a great elation over this victory.'

The next day Jonsson's CO, Sqn Ldr Tony Bartley, made his first claim since arriving in North Africa when he shot down a C.202 over Bone. Tony Jonsson recalled;

'They were doing low-level attacks on our aerodrome. For some inexplicable reason, the one that Tony Bartley shot down was flying upside down at the time!'

——Bitter Opposition, and Weather——

At this time No 81 Sqn under Sqn Ldr 'Ras' Berry moved into Bone (also known as Tingley), where it established itself in primitive and uncomfortable conditions that were not helped by the constant rain and Luftwaffe bombing raids. Among its pilots that would later become aces were Sgts Alan Peart and Larry Cronin, the former commenting;

'Unfortunately, our Spitfire VCs were no match for our opponent's Bf 109Gs, which made our lives a misery. Our main problem was that we were not far away from the main Luftwaffe fighter base at Bizerte, and we were subjected to strafing attacks during the day. To counter the attacks we always had a pair of fighters on patrol over our base and another pair strapped in ready to take-off. In general, my recollection is of a period when one tried hard to defend, do one's job and stay alive.'

It was over Bone that No 111 Sqn's Spitfires saw further action on 17 November when, amongst others, Flt Lt 'Mac' Gilmour downed a Ju 88 for his first success over North Africa. 'Tony' Jonsson was also involved;

'I had been on patrol with two of my companions when a large gaggle of Ju 88s attacked the harbour. We chased them out to sea, and on my third attack on one of them it blew up.'

They were also joined at Bone by No 72 Sqn, and 'Dutch' Hugo soon had them off, as CO Sqn Ldr Bobby Oxspring explained in his memoirs;

'No sooner had we refuelled than "Piet" led No 81 Sqn and us in 72 on a sweep to the Tabarka area. As we climbed out of Bone we sighted a lone Ju 88 pushing his luck as he crossed our track. We poured on the coals in a race to get there first and "Piet" got the edge and bored in on a full quarter attack. His shooting was a sight to behold, as in one long burst his cannon shells raked the enemy from nose to tail. With a momentary fiery explosion, it disintegrated and fell in a shower of bits.'

It was Hugo's 12th victory, whilst in No 72 Sqn others too were making their mark, including Flg Off Owen Hardy, who, on 19 November, destroyed a Bf 109 over Bone to claim his second victory – and his unit's first in North Africa. However, soon afterwards No 72 Sqn lost several aircraft and men when enemy fighters strafed their strip, as one of the pilots noted in his diary;

'Twelve '109s bombed and machine gunned us at 1330 hrs, wiping out eight of our Spits. Krohn got one. Cox hurt.'

On the 26th David Cox, who had four successes, was in a fight near Djedeida, attacking a Bf 109F at 6000 ft. He gave it a long burst, seeing strikes on the engine before the port wing crumpled. This victory made Cox an ace. Another beginning his path to acedom at this time was squadronmate Flt Sgt Roy Hussey, who attacked another Bf 109 from astern. It immediately turned and dived away, with Hussey in hot pursuit, and the fighter shed pieces under his fire before it crashed vertically into a hillside and exploded. As was his style, 'Dutch' Hugo was leading No 72 Sqn on this occasion, and he too shot down a Bf 109. This success meant that he was the first pilot to achieve five victories since the landings earlier in the month.

No 324 Wing CO, Australian Gp Capt Ronnie Lees, got in on the act too, earning him Sqn Ldr Bobby Oxspring's admiration;

'Gp Capt Lees was everywhere urging us to maximum effort. In spite of all his onerous responsibilities he found time to fly with us whenever he could. He was hugely satisfied on one of those trips to weigh into a Savoia 79 bomber, which he destroyed with relish.'

The laurels for this period of heavy fighting went to Don Carlson's No 154 Sqn, however, when his wingman, Flg Off 'Paddy' Chambers, performed one of the outstanding individual feats of the campaign by shooting down four bombers in a single sortie. On 28 November he was patrolling over a convoy off the port of Algiers when five Italian SM.79s approached to bomb Allied shipping. Chambers came in from above and behind and attacked four of them in turn before his aircraft was damaged and he exhausted his ammunition. He had reached acedom in spectacular fashion. Another bomber, claimed as a Dornier but also possibly an SM.79, fell to Flg Off Alan Aikman, who became an ace as well.

No 111 Sqn was in action over Bone the next day, and one of its Canadians, Flg Off Bill Draper, set out on the path to become an ace

Having been damaged when with No 242 Sqn, after repair Spitfire VC ER676/HT-E was issued to No 154 Sqn, with whom it is seen here at Souk el Khemis on 24 April 1943. The fighter had been flown during February by ace Flt Lt Alan Aikman, but it was lost on a bomber escort mission the day after this photograph was taken (via R C B Ashworth)

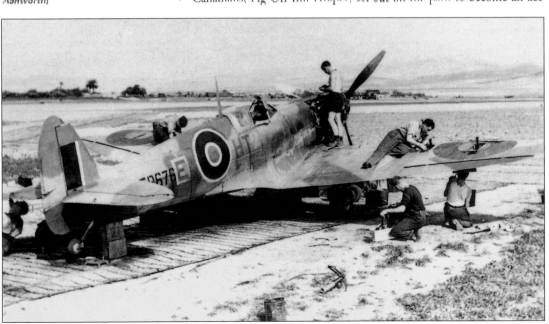

when he shot down a Ju 88 and shared in the destruction of another.

The privations on the ground were compounded by torrential rain, but the stiff enemy opposition continued. Among those in action was Alan Peart of No 81 Sqn;

'I encountered some Italian bombers on 1 December and crept up on a couple that were rather stupidly flying just below a cloud layer. When close enough to open fire, I placed the dot on my reflector sight just ahead of them and pressed the firing button. The bomber shook violently as both cannons and machine guns erupted. It suddenly seemed to stop in mid air, with pieces falling off, and then it went into a steep dive straight into the sea.'

Toronto born Alan Aikman claimed all ten of his victories with No 154 Sqn, rapidly rising to ace status in the heavy air fighting over Algeria in November 1942 (*via R C Sturtivant*)

It was the New Zealander's first step to acedom. That same day the Germans counterattacked in the Teboura area. Elsewhere, during an early morning convoy patrol off Phillippeville, No 242 Sqn's Sgt Mallinson shared in the destruction of what he thought was a Ba.88 reconnaissance aircraft. Later in the day when Bone harbour was attacked by SM.84 bombers of 32° *Stormo* and their Re.2001 escorts, James Mallinson became an ace when he dived on the starboard aircraft in the formation and set both its port and starboard engines alight. The bomber crashed in flames. Sadly, Mallinson's was but a brief glory for on 2 January he was shot down and killed in combat with Bf 109s over Bone.

The heavy action over Algeria and Tunisia in December was to see other Spitfire pilots becoming aces, among them Plt Off 'Robbie' Robertson of No 72 Sqn. On the 3rd he dived on some Fw 190s between Teboura and Djedeida, and despite being attacked by USAAF P-38s, he shot one down. The next day Plt Offs Lindsay and Hamblyn of No 242 Sqn were on a convoy escort when they intercepted five SM.79 torpedo-bombers of 280ª *Squadriglia* off Bizerte. Scotsman Willie Lindsay recounted the encounter to the author;

'We identified them as "Ba.88s" on the same course as ourselves. We attacked and Hamblyn went after a straggler and put it into the sea with one of its engines ablaze. I had gone for the bomber on the extreme right of the formation, and saw hits before it too crashed into the sea. I also attacked another on the right and it too went down, shedding large pieces as it did so. However, I had by this time seen that Hamblyn's Spitfire had been hit and was streaming glycol, so I went to cover him until he bailed out. Much later I learned that the bombers were Savoia 79s, and that four of them had gone down, so we must have got two each. I also discovered later that my unfortunate leader had been rescued by an enemy ship and had become a prisoner.'

This action saw both pilots elevated to ace status.

The Spitfire pilots endured hard and dogged fighting against an experienced and able foe, and December 1942 saw many of them adding considerably to their scores. One such individual was No 81 Sqn's James Walker, who on the 6th became embroiled in a dogfight over Bone with

Italian Re.2001 fighters of 362ª *Squadriglia*. In sharing in the destruction of the aircraft flown by Tenente Pederzoli, he was elevated to ace status. Also reaching this coveted position was fellow Canadian Harry Fenwick, who shared the Re.2001 with Walker and then shot down a Bf 109 for his fifth kill. His Spitfire was also damaged, however, and he again had to force land, this time at Souk el Arba.

Fighter units remained highly mobile throughout this period, as the CO of No 232 Sqn, Sqn Ldr Archie Winskill, recalled;

'We flew in gaggles direct to Phillipeville – we were a fully mobile self-contained unit with tents, mobile kitchens, vehicles and 360 personnel, including our own RAF Regiment for airfield defence.'

One of the RAF's 'characters' in Tunisia was 37-year-old WO 'Chas' Charnock of No 72 Sqn, who on 18 December was seen to shoot down a Bf 109 and an Fw 190 prior to his own Spitfire being hit and set on fire by the Fw 190 flown by *experte* Leutnant Erich Rudorffer of II./JG 2. Having crash-landed, a wounded Charnock quickly made contact with some local Arabs and bribed them to assist him back to Allied lines, where, after treatment he was able to rejoin the squadron. Upon rejoining No 72 Sqn he discovered that he was to be commissioned, and also awarded a DFC! Sqn Ldr Oxspring said of the former Harrovian, who was by some margin the oldest fighter pilot in the theatre, 'Chas was a remarkable character. A product of Harrow and Cranwell, he had been court martialled and dismissed the Service for a low flying offence in 1930, but as a natural aviator he ranked with the best.'

In the same action 'Robbie' Robertson made his final claim when he also shot down a Bf 109. Bobby Oxspring recalled the fight over Beja;

'A cannon shell slashed into "Robbie's" cockpit, blasting a splinter of debris through one of his eyes. Half blinded, he made a courageous crash-landing. He'd done a great job, but in spite of much treatment he eventually lost his right eye.'

Oxspring summarised the experiences of most units in this period;

'Almost every mission resulted in a clash of opposing fighters. In this environment No 72 Sqn had a ball. In four weeks it accounted for 21 enemy aircraft destroyed and eight probables.'

Towards year-end things began to improve for the RAF fighter units, but the same could not be said for the recognition skills of the USAAF pilots, as No 242 Sqn's Willie Lindsay discovered on Boxing Day;

'It was a bloody American that shot me down. I was in a slow descent, getting ready to land at the nearby airstrip, and he simply got behind and above me and fired! Fortunately, I was dragged out of the crashed aircraft by a native boy and his father, who then loaded me onto their donkey and carted me off to the RAF base. I am still suffering from the effects of the shrapnel in both feet, and require the assistance of an elbow crutch to get around, but at least I am still here to tell the story.'

ON TOWARDS TUNIS

New Year's Day 1943 fell on a Friday, and at 1030 hrs No 242 Sqn's base at Bone was the subject of a surprise attack by Bf 109s quickly followed by a second wave of Ju 87s with a fighter escort and then a third wave of Fw 190s. Among those from No 242 Sqn that scrambled was Flt Lt Douglas Benham. The unit's ORB described the subsequent events;

'Flt Lt Benham dived on a Fw 190 and fired cannon and machine guns, seeing enemy aircraft go into deck five miles southeast of Morris. Attacked another Fw 190 at 12,000 ft, seeing strikes all over fuselage. Little later Flt Lt Benham saw 15 aircraft in cloud flying east and then saw four more flying from west and two from north, all of which joined up with 15 Ju 87s. Flt Lt Benham attacked one of the Ju 87s at 1000 ft with five-second burst and saw enemy aircraft go into the sea off Cape Rosa. Having used up all his cannon, he sprayed two Ju 87s wth machine gun fire until ammunition exhausted, and saw definite strikes all over two enemy aircraft.'

Benham thus also became a Spitfire ace over Tunisia. However, No 242 Sqn also suffered several losses during this engagement, and the next day four more Spitfires fell. Among those lost to Bf 109s was Sgt James Mallinson, who since the landings had claimed 4.5 victories. A few days later Archie Winskill's No 232 Sqn also arrived at Bone;

'My logbook records a patrol from Bone on 4 January 1943 when Sgt J S Ekbery – my No 2 – and I intercepted a Ju 88. We both attacked and it disappeared into low cloud billowing black smoke. We could not claim it for sure, but HMS *Aurora* picked up wreckage of a Ju 88 some miles off the coast and brought it into Bone harbour a few days later. On 18 January it was my turn for a dunking. I led ten Spitfires on a sweep over the Matyear area and G J Lynes shot down an Fw 190, but my aircraft was hit by flak and I was forced to ditch and swim ashore.'

No 111 Sqn, led by Sqn Ldr Tony Bartley (who had claimed his 13th, and final, victory on 28 December 1942), now flew more escort missions for fighter-bombers, and these resulted in increased enemy contact. One such sortie was performed on 22 January, and it saw Icelandic 'Tony' Jonsson claim his final success over Africa;

'We were met by a gaggle of enemy fighters determined to intercept the Hurricanes. As was usual in such situations, the squadron split up into small groups and individual combats developed. German fighters seemed to be all over the sky, and each time I was about to open fire on one of them my wingman would warn me to break left or right – Dennis Moss did an excellent job. In one of our tight orbits I saw cannon shells from a Me 109 hit the forward part of his aeroplane, causing the engine to seize. At that moment I became aware of tracer bullets shooting past me, and I had to take sharp avoiding action. Just at that moment I caught sight of a Me 109 far below me heading for Dennis. I wasted no time in diving down towards the enemy and I quickly caught up with him. By the time he was getting within range of Dennis, the '109's wings more than spanned my reflector sight and I pressed the firing button. The Messerschmitt exploded and fell burning to the ground.'

Sadly, when force landing in the rocky hills, Plt Off Moss' Spitfire burst into flames and he was killed. The Icelander also described a slightly less conventional victory on 26 January by a fellow future ace;

'Bill Draper downed a Fw 190 in an unusual way. He and the enemy attacked each other head-on at a combined speed of about 700 mph, and both obstinately refused to give way. At the last moment the German went over the top and his propeller shattered against the tail of Bill's Spitfire. This happened at low altitude and the Focke-Wulf hit the ground, while Bill managed to nurse his damaged Spitfire back to base.'

The CO of No 232 Sqn in 1942-43 was Sqn Ldr Archie Winskill, who, having been shot down in January 1943, had to swim ashore into enemy-held territory and evade back to Allied lines. Winskill became an ace in early April when he led his squadron on an interception of a Stuka raid, shooting down one Ju 87 and sharing in the destruction of a second dive-bomber (*Sir Archie Winskill*)

Two days later, however, the squadron suffered a severe blow when 13-victory ace Flt Lt Edward Mortimer-Rose collided on take-off with Wg Cdr 'Sheep' Gilroy and was killed, although the latter managed to bail out.

By the beginning of February 1943 the Germans were still firmly fixed in northern Tunisia, where General Hans von Arnim could muster about 100,000 men and where every attempt by the British to advance had been driven back. Elsewhere, Free French and American troops pressed to threaten the coastal plain, and thus the rear of Rommel's position further to the south, but these advances had also been checked. As a result, air fighting continued unabated, especially following Rommel's successful move against US forces in the Kasserine Pass between 19 and 25 February.

On 26 January 1943 Flg Off Bill Draper (left) of No 111 Sqn shot down two Fw 190s near Souk el Arba, the second of which he engaged 'head-to-head' and as the Focke-Wulf pulled up its propeller clipped the top of Draper's rudder, before crashing into the ground. Having been credited with his fourth victory, a relieved Draper shows the damaged rudder to a Canadian colleague (*via T Hooton*)

By now the first Spitfire IXs had begun arriving on the Tunisian front with No 81 Sqn, and it was in one of these on 31 January that future Rhodesian ace Flg Off William Maguire made his first claim over North Africa when, over Tabarka, he shot down a Bf 109G of I./JG 53. Wg Cdr 'Ras' Berry claimed another on this date, his kill being the penultimate of his 24 victories, and first as leader of No 322 Wing.

Berry had been replaced as No 81 Sqn's CO by fellow high-scoring ace Sqn Ldr Colin Gray, who had already amassed 19 victories in the UK. His first action of this tour came on 22 February when leading a flight on patrol with No 154 Sqn. Off Cap Rosa, four Bf 109s were sighted, and in the ensuing battle Gray claimed a probable kill, having seen strikes on the fighter's wings and tail before his cannon jammed.

Several days earlier, the heavy fighting around the Kasserine Pass had begun, and it reached a climax on 20 February. Having forced a way through the Pass, the *Afrika Korps* renewed its advance the following day. Its panzers met with stiff British resistance in the south, and heavy losses slow their progress. Appalling weather also limited any air support for either side. However, the day Colin Gray made his North African debut proved to be the turning point in the battle, and with his lines of communication extended and vulnerable, Rommel went onto the defensive. He was particularly concerned about the impending Allied assault on the Mareth Line in the south.

Over Algiers, 22 February also saw the first Spitfire victory for Sqn Ldr Micky Rook's recently equipped No 43 Sqn when Plt Off Wills shot down a reconnoitring Ju 88 from 2.(F)/122 off the coast. The Germans quietly began withdrawing from Kasserine on the 23rd, and over the

On 19 February 1943 Flt Lt David Cox (right) received a DFC. Here, he is congratulated on his award by his CO in No 72 Sqn, fellow ace Sqn Ldr Bobby Oxspring, who by that stage of the war had himself amassed a dozen victories. Oxspring had also been awarded a second bar to the DFC at the same time Cox received his decoration (*D S G R Cox*)

In the spring of 1943 Spitfire IXs began arriving in Tunisia, some re-equipping No 72 Sqn. One such aircraft was EN298/RN-B, which was assigned to Flt Lt David Cox. Already with 5.5 kills to his name, Cox used the fighter to down a Bf 109 over Medjez el Bab on 3 April for what proved to be his final victory. He also claimed a probable and two damaged with EN298. Cox ended the war leading a Spitfire Wing in Burma (*D S G R Cox*)

Front during an escort mission Canadian Flt Lt George Hill of No 111 Sqn shot down a Bf 109. He would become an ace in little over a week.

The Allies reoccupied Kasserine on 25 February, and that afternoon a quartet of Spitfires from No 232 Sqn patrolling over Bone harbour were directed to Cap Rosa, where they spotted an enemy reconnaissance aircraft at 10,000 ft escorted by a dozen Bf 109s. In the subsequent fight Sgt Whiting claimed a probable and a damaged, although Sgt Joe Ekbery had to ditch his badly shot up aircraft but was saved – the future ace was *experte* Hauptmann Tonne's 111th victory. That same day No 72 Sqn returned to action, having re-equipped with Spitfire IXs. The latter caused Sqn Ldr Oxspring to wax lyrical about them;

'It was a sheer joy to feel the surging power of the Spitfire Mk IX over the Mk V. We hadn't realised how much we'd missed it since Biggin Hill days six months earlier!'

Bobby Oxspring also made Flt Lts David Cox and 'Dan' Daniel his new flight commanders, saying 'I was fortunate to have "Coxy" and "Danny" in 72. They were largely responsible for the squadron's dynamic record in the Tunisian campaign'.

With the fighting around Mareth beginning, in the north the enemy began a thrust toward Beja. Axis flak, as ever, was a permanent danger, as No 243 Sqn's new CO, Sqn Ldr James Walker, found to his cost when he was hit. He managed to crash land in Allied lines. Fighter-bomber escorts to help counter the flak threat continued, and in the Beja area on 28 February Sqn Ldr Bobby Oxspring claimed his penultimate victory;

'Returning from a mission, we found No 152 Sqn on airfield defence battling it out with some Me 109Gs. Having the height and speed 72 mixed in, scattering the formations into individual dogfights. One '109 climbed away east out of the melee, and I followed with my wingman, "Red" Hunter. We hung on until we reached 19,000 ft, at which point the supercharger cut in, sending me close underneath the '109's tail. I let fly and white glycol streamed from the engine as the canopy peeled away and the pilot bailed out. He dropped to my left and I saw his parachute blossom. A second later he fell out of the harness and careered earthward, leaving a flapping canopy behind. "Poor bastard" I thought.'

Similar missions continued into early March, and on the first day of the new month No 243 Sqn saw action with Bf 109s of JG 53. Plt Off M Hume shot one of the fighters down to claim the unit's first victory in Africa. Three days later Sqn Ldr Walker made his first claim with his new squadron when he damaged a Bf 109 near Sedjenane. However, the Spitfire Vs were by now having real problems countering the Luftwaffe's latest fighters, as No 232 Sqn CO Archie Winskill recalled;

'The trouble was of course that with our Mk VCs we were completely outclassed by both the Me 109G and the Fw 190, so No 232 Sqn in North Africa was not really in the fighter v fighter

league. Yet despite being at a disadvantage, we did remarkably well. At Bone we did the best we could in the fighter defence role, but the best pickings went to No 81 Sqn equipped with the Spit IX. When we moved into the Souk el Arba valley we were then located on the main thrust line, and our main roles were providing close escort for USAAF bombers and attacking ground targets – road convoys and airfields – with our two cannons and four 0.303s. Of course one had to be very, very careful as the German light/medium flak was devastating.'

Rommel's last throw came in mid March, after which the Allied armies began to close the ring. Progress on the northern front was at first slow, but above them the Spitfire squadrons kept the skies clear of enemy aircraft, despite the poor weather. On 23 March No 81 Sqn's Sqn Ldr Colin Gray shot down a C.202 to claim his first victory over North Africa, then two days later, during a dogfight west of Beja, he brought down a Bf 109 that was attacking another Spitfire. Coming in from above and behind, Gray saw his cannon shells strike the fighter's port wing root. One leg of the undercarriage dropped and then it streamed glycol, forcing the pilot to bail out.

No 72 Sqn had more success during a sweep on 26 March when Flt Lts 'Dan' Daniel and Owen Hardy each destroyed a Bf 109. Daniel's victory elevated him to acedom, while Hardy's kill was his sixth, and last. There was still action to be had back in Algeria too, for on 29 March Flg Off Willie Lindsay claimed his final victory when, north of Phillippeville, he shared in the destruction of an He 111 from I./KG 26.

EVACUATION

With the Mareth Line effectively turned and the Allies advancing in the north, Axis forces found themselves in increasingly desperate straits. With Allied control of the sea routes, the enemy increasingly relied on air transport to fly supplies in from Italy. To counter this, the Allies instigated Operation *Flax*, which would inflict grievous losses on German and Italian transport units. The fight for mastery of the skies continued throughout this period too, No 145 Sqn's Polish Fighting Team seeing action on 2 April when Sqn Ldr Stanislaw Skalski was engaged north of El Hamma;

'I got in behind a '109 after diving to 6000-7000 ft, firing from 200 yards astern. After my third attack there was an explosion behind the cockpit and a cloud of white smoke. The aircraft spun and hit the sea.'

The following day Colin Gray was also in a dogfight near Tunis;

'I saw an aircraft coming towards me at high speed, and as he flashed past I recognised an Me 109G2. He also obviously recognised me as hostile because he immediately pulled into a screaming left-hand turn and attempted to dogfight. This was a big mistake because there was no way a '109 could turn inside a Spitfire. It took only a few minutes to get on his tail and a short burst with cannon and machine guns produced much smoke, glycol and large chunks falling off. Jerry bailed out and flashed by me going down, although his parachute appeared to stream and it did not open before the poor beggar hit the ground.'

Flax began on the 5th, and No 93 Sqn on a sweep led by Gilroy saw Plt Off Stan Browne, a former medical student, shoot down a Bf 109 to take his first step to acedom on a day when the enemy suffered heavy

In the spring of 1943 No 145 Sqn was reinforced by a flight of experienced pilots – the Polish Fighting Team – led by Sqn Ldr Stanislaw Skalski, who was to claim three victories over North Africa *(via W Matusiak)*

losses. Two days later it was the turn of Archie Winskill's No 232 Sqn to be busy;

'Our area of course was Bizerte/Tunis and the main routes to Mateur. On the evening of 7 April we encountered a large formation of Ju 87s and we managed to down several. I saw one that I attacked jettison its bombs before crashing on fire. I remember that Woodhill and I got another, and I think the squadron got four in total. I am quite sure that 232 was very effective indeed, particularly when, at the very end, the Germans were trying to evacuate as much as they could by air from Bizerte and Tunis in the Ju 52 and Me 323 transports.'

Winskill's Ju 87 victories were his first successes in North Africa, and they had made him an ace.

It was the vulnerable transports that were the main priority, however, and on 16 April three Spitfire IXs from No 92 Sqn on a sweep over the Cape Bon Peninsula spotted 18 SM.82s low over the sea. Five were destroyed despite the fighter escort, as Neville Duke recalled;

'When we were over the Cape, I saw a large number of transport aircraft low down, and I called the "Wingco" and went down. They were Savoia 82s, large three-engined jobs – about 18 of them. The first one I attacked I was going so fast I couldn't get more than a short

Having downed a Bf 109G over Tunis on 6 April to claim his 20th kill, No 81 Sqn's Sqn Ldr Colin Gray tells the groundcrew of his success as he walks away from Spitfire IX EN445. He said of the action 'Jerry bailed out and flashed by me going down' (*C F Gray*)

Skalski's usual aircraft was Mk IX EN459/ZX-1, but on 6 April it was flown by his fellow Polish ace Flt Lt Eugeniusz Horbaczewski in a combat when he shot down a Bf 109 for his sixth victory. He was then hit but managed to force land at Gabes, where EN459 is seen being dismantled for repair (*R Freeman*)

An SM.82 and four massive Me 323s fly in formation across the Mediterranean in a vain attempt to re-supply Axis forces in Tunisia. They suffered very heavy losses to Allied fighters (particularly Spitfires) in the attempt (*SAAF*)

On 2 April Lt 'Robbie' Robinson of No 1 Sqn SAAF was flying ER171/AX-D *Maureen* when he claimed his fourth victory by shooting down a Bf 109G. He had 'made ace' by month-end (*SAAF Museum via R C Sturtivant*)

burst in. I then attacked another after throttling right back, letting him have everything. Closing right up, I just skimmed over the top of him, having seen my shells explode all over him. He flew into the sea with a terrific splash, and I had a fleeting vision of pieces of cowling etc. flying up with a sheet of spray.'

Duke quickly shot down a second SM.82, and these were his last victories over North Africa for he left for a rest soon afterwards.

This engagement was far from one-sided, however, as during the course of the interception No 244 Wing leader and 16-victory ace Wg Cdr 'Widge' Gleed was lost. He was subsequently replaced by Sqn Ldr Peter Olver from No 1 Sqn SAAF. And it was this unit that amongst others made many claims during the great Axis transport massacre off Cape Bon on the 22nd when the Luftwaffe committed a consignment of petrol to huge six-engined Messerschmitt Me 323s. Intercepted over the Gulf of Tunis by a large force of Spitfires and Kittyhawks, the enemy transports were mown down almost to the last aircraft. The escorting fighters were also badly mauled, with Lt 'Robbie' Robinson of No 1 Sqn SAAF destroying two Bf 109s to become an ace. One of his colleagues wrote;

'The transport aircraft were sighted flying just above the water towards Tunis. They were six-engined powered gliders, Me 323s, each capable of carrying 14 tons, and were flying in a great vic of 15, with a smaller vic of 5 inside it. It is estimated that the transport aircraft had a scattered escort of ten Me 109s and MC 202s. A great slaughter now began. Our total claims were six Me 323s and two Me 109Fs, all downed in flames.'

On 24 April No 72 Sqn's Flg Off 'Chem' Le Cheminant became the latest Spitfire pilot to achieve acedom over North Africa when he blew the wing off a Bf 109, whilst the next day (25 April) New Zealander Sgt Alan Peart claimed his second victory;

'I latched onto a ME 109 which climbed hard, with me hot on his tail. He either didn't know I was there or he thought he could outperform me, because he just kept climbing and turning ahead of me. I put in one burst with cannons and machine guns, which hit him, but didn't seem to do any discernable serious damage. Just as I was ready to fire again, his canopy flew off and the pilot bailed out, his body just missing my wing.'

On May Day Flg Off Bill Draper of No 111 Sqn achieved his fifth, and final, victory when he destroyed a Bf 109 near Ras Zebib. The next day No 81 Sqn's Flg Off William Maguire also 'made ace' when he too shot down a Bf 109 for his fifth victory.

Surviving Axis forces were by now confined to a small area and facing certain defeat, and the end finally came on the 13th when Marshal Giovanni Messe surrendered Army Group Africa (numbering a quarter of a million troops). This capitulation prompted 18th Army Group commander Gen Harold Alexander to wire Prime Minister Winston Churchill with the message 'All enemy resistance has ceased. We are masters of the North African shore'.

During January 1943 No 81 Sqn re-equipped with Spitfire IXs, and it used these aircraft to successfully challenge the Luftwaffe for aerial supremacy over Tunisia. One such machine was EN204, which as FL-E was used on ANZAC Day (25 April 1943) by New Zealander Sgt Alan Peart to claim his second victory. The fighter later became FL-L, as seen here, and was the regular mount of future ace WO Larry Cronin. It was also flown by several other successful pilots in No 81 Sqn, including Sgt Don Rathwell and Plt Off Bill Caldecott (*A Peart*)

No 145 Sqn CO Sqn Ldr Lance Wade, nicknamed 'Wildcat', ruefully examines the damage to his wingtip at Goubrane North after combat over the Gulf of Tunis on 6 May 1943 (*JSCSC*)

FINAL SKIRMISHES

The end of the campaign in Tunisia was not the last action the Spitfire was to see over Africa, however, as enemy bombers still threatened Allied shipping. Some Algerian-based Free French units also began receiving Spitfire Vs, including GC II/7 'Nice' under Cdt Marie Papin-Labazordiere, who had claimed three victories during the Battle of France. Further east in Egypt the special flight of No 103 MU continued to counter enemy high altitude intrusions, Flt Lt Mike Cooper-Slipper damaging the Ju 88 of 2.(F)/123 flown by Unteroffizier Lotar Rohrich on 15 June, the ace noting of his final combat claim;

'Closed in at 50 yards, hitting enemy aircraft port side and engine. Enemy aircraft rolled to the left.

Held back for the defence of Egypt following the Allied advance westward, No 80 Sqn re-equipped with Spitfire VCs (including JG839/EY-S) in the spring of 1943. A number of successful pilots served with the unit at the time, including CO Sqn Ldr Ron Bary, who flew this aircraft on occasion (*C W Jarold*)

Got burst from 70 yards, opened fire but port cannon did not fire and I could not keep sights on enemy aircraft. Followed enemy aircraft to sea level – short bursts with starboard cannon. After first attack, enemy's port undercarriage leg fell out and went back up again.'

Later in the summer the Flight, under Flt Lt 'Shorty' West, was attached to No 80 Sqn at Savoia. In mid August he damaged a reconnaissance Bf 109 and on the 24th, when flying JK980, West shot down a Bf 109 to claim his sixth victory.

There continued to be occasional skirmishes for North African-based Spitfires such as on 26 November, when GC II/7's Lt Guy Bouttier shot down a Do 217 off Bougie, in Algeria. In the same raid Adj Charles Leroy downed an Fw 200, as did Lt Roger Perrier for his first victory. Also claiming during the same action was Lt Raoul Rebiere, who was credited with a Do 217 for his fifth victory. No 32 Sqn, which had recently received Spitfire HF VIIIs, claimed a Ju 88 in early December, and there continued to be a trickle of successes into 1944, with Roger Perrier bagging an 'Me 210' off Algiers in late April.

Probably the last victory by a Spitfire based in French North Africa came on 3 July 1944 when a Ju 88T-1 from 1.(F)/33 was shot down by WO Hally of 'C' Flight, No 256 Sqn (formerly the Gibraltar Defence Flight) 25 miles to the north of the port of Oran in Algeria. Hally was flying a Spitfire VIII at the time.

The High Altitude Flight of No 103 MU continued to counter high-flying intrusions into Egypt by the Luftwaffe. In July 1943 Flt Lt 'Shorty' West, who already had five victories to his name, led a detachment to Savoia, in Libya, where it was parented by the resident No 94 Sqn. West, second from the right, is thought to have been flying this Spitfire IX (JK980) when he claimed his final victory on 24 August – a Bf 109 that was on a reconnaissance flight off the Libyan coast (*Ian Simpson*)

1
Spitfire VB AB326/ZX-A of Flt Lt J J P Sabourin, No 145 Sqn, Gambut, Libya, 1 June 1942

2
Spitfire VC ER502/UF-X of Flg Off M R B Ingram, No 601 'County of London' Sqn, El Nogra, Libya, December 1942

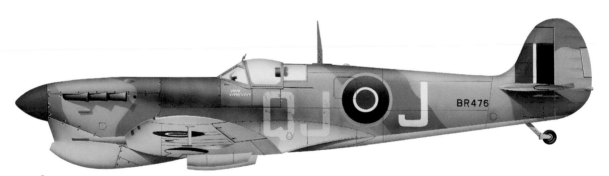

3
Spitfire VB BR476/QJ-J of Sqn Ldr J H Wedgewood, No 92 Sqn, LG 173, Egypt, August-October 1942

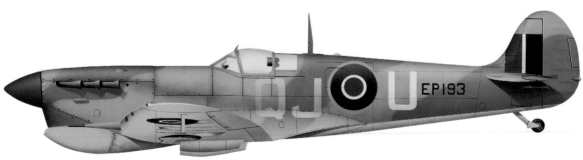

4
Spitfire VC EP193/QJ-U of Flt Lt J L Waddy, No 92 Sqn, LG 173, Egypt, 22 October 1942

5
Spitfire VC EP690/AX-A of Maj P C R Metelerkamp, No 1 Sqn SAAF, LG 05, Egypt, 27 November 1942

6
Spitfire VC ER676/B-E of Flt Lt D I Benham, No 242 Sqn, Bone, Algeria, December 1942

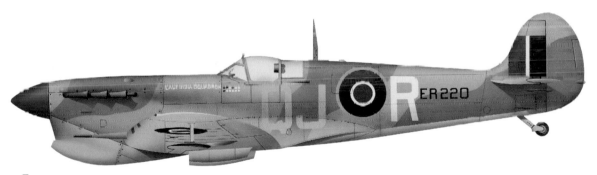

7
Spitfire VC ER220/QJ-R of Flg Off N F Duke, No 92 Sqn, Hamraiet and Wadi Sirru, Libya, January 1943

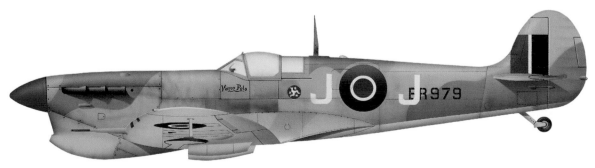

8
Spitfire VC ER979/J-J of Sgt F Campbell, No 93 Sqn, Souk el Khemis, Algeria, January-March 1943

9
Spitfire VB ER773/RS-J of Sqn Ldr S C Norris, No 33 Sqn, Bersis, Libya, February 1943

10
Spitfire VC ER676/HT-E of Flt Lt A F Aikman, No 154 Sqn, Maison Blanche, Algeria, 26 February 1943

11
Spitfire IX EN116/RN-A of Sqn Ldr R W Oxspring, No 72 Sqn, Souk el Khemis, Algeria, March-April 1943

12
Spitfire VC ER228/ZX-S of Flt Lt J S Taylor, No 145 Sqn, Ben Gardane, Tunisia, 7 March 1943

13
Spitfire IX EN298/RN-B of Flt Lt D G S R Cox, No 72 Sqn, Souk el Khemis, Algeria, March-April 1943

14
Spitfire VC JK101/FT-Z of Sqn Ldr M Rook, No 43 Sqn, Jemappes, Algeria, April 1943

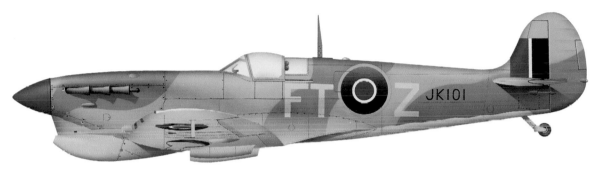

15
Spitfire IX EN315/ZX-6 of Flt Lt E Horbaczewski, No 145 Sqn Polish Fighting Team, La Fouconnerie, Tunisia, April 1943

16
Spitfire VC ER807/SN-E of Sqn Ldr J E Walker, No 243 Sqn, Souk el Khemis, Algeria, 10 April 1943

17
Spitfire VC JG871/L-E of Sgt L A Smith, No 152 Sqn, Setif, Algeria, 14 and 21 April 1943

18
Spitfire IX EN204/FL-L of Sgt L A Cronin, No 81 Sqn, Souk el Khemis and Protville, Algeria, May 1943

19
Spitfire VC JG839/EY-S of Sqn Ldr R E Bary, No 80 Sqn, Idku, Egypt, 23 May 1943

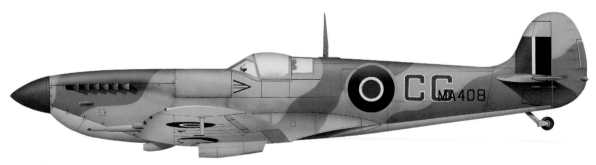

20
Spitfire IX MA408/CG of Wg Cdr C F Gray, No 322 Wing, Lentini East, Sicily, August 1943

21
Spitfire VC JK322/FL-4 of Flg Off A M Peart, No 81 Sqn, Takali, Malta, 16 July 1943

22
Spitfire IX JK980 of Flt Lt J G West, No 103 MU attached to No 94 Sqn, Savoia, Libya, 24 August 1943

23
Spitfire IX MA454/UM-V of Flt Lt G T Baynham, No 152 Sqn, Lentini East, Sicily, 27 August 1943

24
Spitfire IX LZ950/EF-F of Flt Lt W A Olmstead, No 232 Sqn, Montecorvino, Sicily, 11 and 24 September 1943

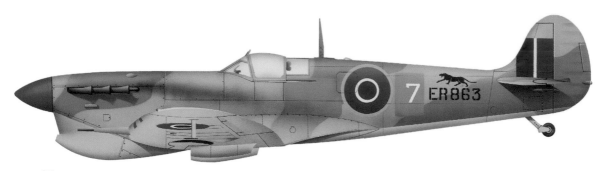

25
Spitfire VC ER863 '7' of Cdt H Hugo, *Groupe de Chasse* II/7, Ajaccio, Corsica, October 1943

26
Spitfire IX EN459/HN-D of Flt Lt I F Kennedy, No 93 Sqn, Tortorolla, Italy, 15 October 1943

27
Spitfire VC JK465/GN-X of Sqn Ldr E N Woods, No 249 Sqn, Grottaglie, Italy, October-November 1943

28
Spitfire VC LZ943/BQ-B of Flg Off D H McBurnie, No 451 Sqn, El Daba, Egypt, 18 November 1943

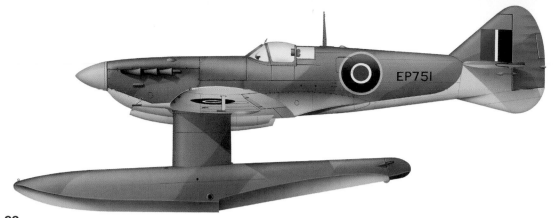

29
Spitfire VB EP751 of Flt Lt W R M Lindsay, Floatplane Flight, No 71 OTU, Fanora, Egypt, December 1943

30
Spitfire VIII JF627/AN-M of Flg Off G E Horricks, No 417 Sqn, Canne, Italy, 9 January 1944

31
Spitfire VIII JF476/QJ-D of Lt J H Gasson, No 92 Sqn, Marcianise, Italy, 16 February 1944

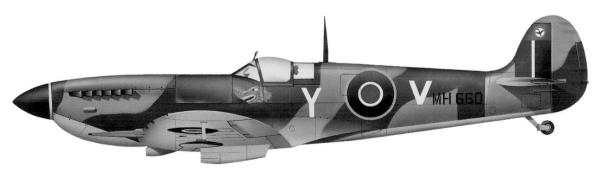

32
Spitfire IX MH660/V-Y of Flt Lt W E Schrader, No 1435 Sqn, Brindisi, Italy, 4 March 1944

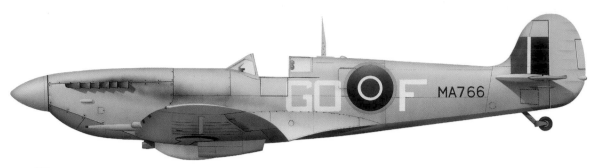

33
Spitfire IX MA766/GO-F of Sqn Ldr R G Foskett, No 94 Sqn, Bu Amud, Egypt, 6 June 1944

34
Spitfire IX PL348/TM of Wg Cdr E J Morris, No 251 Wing, Cuers, France, September 1944

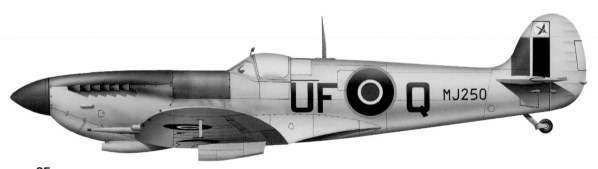

35
Spitfire IX MJ250/UF-Q of Flt Lt D Ibbotson, No 601 'County of London' Sqn, Fano, Italy, July-November 1944

36
Spitfire VIII JF880/AN-U of Flt Lt K R Linton, No 417 Sqn, Bellaria, Italy, 14 March 1945

ACROSS THE MEDITERRANEAN

Part of the Allied grand strategy after securing North Africa was to make the first return to 'Fortress Europe' via its so-called 'soft underbelly' – Italy. Planning for this phase proceeded apace, with the first objective being to secure the island of Sicily. For this operation Malta would prove an essential stepping stone, but it was also critical that the Italian island fortresses of Lampedusa and Pantelleria in the Sicilian Narrows be neutralised. Operations against these islands began almost immediately, involving units from North Africa and Malta.

It was during the Pantellaria operations that the newly equipped French GC II/7 had its first success with the Spitfire when, on 11 June, Sgt Chef Louis Kahn claimed an Fw 190 and his colleague Adj Constantin Feldzer bagged a Ju 88, as he described;

'What good luck! It was a gift of God on a blue tray. It was mine, this Ju 88. I just had to make a slight change in the course of my dive, so it was no longer a dot in the sky but an aeroplane growing in the middle of my gunsight. Wait a split second to be sure not to miss, and with my body shaking I fire one long burst with all my guns – the aeroplane shakes and the smell of cordite invades the cockpit. Just in time to see the explosion, and I was already 300 ft below and well in front of the blazing Ju 88.'

Shortly before Feldzer's kill, the first elements of No 322 Wing, now led by Wg Cdr Colin Gray, moved across to Malta, and it was he who opened the wing's score in this new theatre on the 14th;

'I dived on a '109 and fired from 200 yards, observing cannon strikes on the fuselage. There was a large explosion behind the cockpit, petrol spewed out and the aeroplane finally caught fire.'

His victim is believed to have been Feldwebel Engelbert Hofmann of 6./JG 53. That same day more Spitfires from Nos 92, 417 and 1 SAAF Sqns transferred to Malta ahead of the Sicilian operation, which began with the surrender of Pantelleria and Lampedusa. During a B-24 escort to Sicily with No 232 Sqn on 17 June, Gray shot down a C.202. Attacks continued with increasing intensity as the date for the invasion approached.

By the end of June three RAF Spitfire wings were temporarily based on Malta, all commanded and led by aces – No 244 Wing had Gp Capt Brian Kingcome and Wg Cdr

A 'pair of aces'! Wg Cdr Brian Kingcome, the Wing Leader of No 244 Wing, meets Maj Frank Hill of the Spitfire-equipped 31st FG at Termini in late August. Both men achieved acedom flying the Spitfire (*F A Hill*)

Between April and October 1943 Sqn Ldr 'Rosie' Mackie of No 243 Sqn flew 180 hours in Spitfire VC JK715/SN-A and also claimed eight victories with it over Tunisia and Sicily (*E D Mackie*)

With a total of 23 victories, including 16 in North Africa and the Mediterranean, Sqn Ldr 'Rosie' Mackie was one of the leading New Zealand pilots of the war. He later commanded No 92 Sqn in Italy and led a Tempest Wing in Northwest Europe (*E D Mackie*)

Peter Olver, No 322 Wing Gp Capt 'Dutch' Hugo and Wg Cdr Colin Gray and No 324 Wing Gp Capt 'Sheep' Gilroy and Wg Cdr 'Cocky' Dundas. Most of the squadrons were led by aces at this time as well.

A typical mission for this period was flown by No 111 Sqn on 3 July, the unit providing aircraft for the escort (led by Wg Cdr Dundas) that was charged with protecting fighter-bombers sent to attack Biscari. As they pulled away from the target, the latter were attacked by 20+ Bf 109s and C.202s, and in the resulting dogfight No 111 Sqn's CO, Sqn Ldr George Hill, downed a Messerschmitt – probably flown by Unteroffizier Walter Reinicke of 7./JG 53 – for his 13th success. However, five-kill ace Flt Sgt Frank Mellor was hit by Bf 109s, as Dundas described;

'We were attacked and my companion's aeroplane was damaged. Luckily, we were by that time crossing over the coast and the enemy fighters pulled away. I saw a thin trail of white smoke streaking out from the Spitfire beside me. I called my No 2 and he replied that his engine temperature was already rising. Sadly, Mellor crashed into the sea and was lost.'

The following day Sqn Ldr 'Rosie' Mackie, flying his regular aircraft JK715/SN-A, led No 243 Sqn to cover B-17s attacking Catania. As the bombers came off target, six Bf 109s appeared and a 'free for all' soon developed;

'I saw approximately six ME 109s at 26,000 ft, and they attacked myself and my No 2. After evasive action I found myself in a suitable position to attack a '109 that was approaching from my starboard side. I fired three deflection bursts, the last from a range of approximately 70 yards. I saw cannon and machine gun strikes all over the cockpit and fuselage. The enemy aircraft burst into flames. I last saw it at 25,000 ft going down vertically in flames with black smoke pouring from it.'

Mackie was back over the island escorting B-17s once again on the 5th, when he got behind a Bf 109 and claimed his tenth victory;

'I saw an ME 109, line astern, and fired cannon from a range of 100 yards, breaking off to avoid a collision. Just before I broke away I saw cannon strikes on the fuselage and wings. The enemy aircraft rolled on its back and went down streaming glycol. I saw it crash and burst into flames just north of Palazzolo.'

Also in the action on this occasion was no less a person then Major Johannes 'Macki' Steinhoff, *Kommodore* of JG 77, who vividly described being on the receiving end of a Spitfire attack;

On 8 July 1943, two days before the landings on Sicily, No 72 Sqn's Plt Off Roy Hussey achieved acedom by shooting down a Bf 109 over Comiso. He had claimed four more victories by month-end (*via C F Shores*)

'There was a thud against the fuselage and I wrenched my head round. Looking past the armour plate, I saw a Spitfire in a steep turn a few yards behind. Smoke from his tracers groped towards me like fingers. My engine stuttered violently. Bullets shattered against the armour plate behind my head with appalling cracks. I half rolled and went into a vertical dive.'

Another victim of the action was 20-victory ace Capitano Franco Luccini of 10° *Gruppo*.

The following evening, during an escort to Gerbini, No 232 Sqn's Flt Sgt Joe Ekbery (in JK365/EF-D) spotted a lone Bf 109 – probably that of Unteroffizier Rolf Daum – and, following it down, sent it crashing into the ground to claim his second victory. He was commissioned the following day. Also recently commissioned was No 72 Sqn's Plt Off Roy Hussey, who, over Comiso on 8 July, achieved acedom when he shot down a Bf 109G. He went on to achieve even greater success following the landings.

INVASION

On the afternoon of 9 July a great mass of ships and landing craft assembled off Malta carrying the British 8th and American 7th Armies, which moved under strong air and naval escort towards Sicily. The landings began at 0400 hrs on the 10th, and they were successful. Throughout the day Allied fighters patrolled over the beaches and the mass of shipping lying off shore, but attacks from the Luftwaffe and *Regia Aeronautica* were less than expected. Nevertheless, 13 Axis aircraft were claimed destroyed, but at a cost of 11 Spitfires shot down or missing.

At Luqa serving with No 92 Sqn at this time was 2Lt John Gasson of the SAAF, who recalled;

'We carried out offensive sweeps over Catania, Comiso and the Gerbini landing grounds until the invasion of Sicily on 10 July. We were the first unit to patrol over our forces, and on the day the landings took place we destroyed a Ju88 (and I damaged another) over the Pachino peninsula. This was the first time I had had contact with the enemy.'

The Ju 88 destroyed refers to Flt Lt 'Doc' Savage's fifth victory, and its demise was witnessed by Canadian ace Flg Off Milt Jowsey;

'I saw Flt Lt Savage shoot down one Ju 88, and while in pursuit of another at about 10,000 ft he was shot down by Royal Navy flak.'

Savage was unable to bail out and was killed. Also shot down was six-victory Rhodesian ace Flg Off 'Dicky' Dicks-Sherwood, who recounted his story to journalist Richard McMillan at the time;

'I was patrolling near Augusta, flying top cover in a Spitfire IX, and I became slightly separated from the main formation. As I went into a turn, I looked up and saw five Me 109s flying for position up-sun and I reported them to the rest of the formation. The Jerries peeled off and came down, hitting me with explosive bullets. Rounds hit the wing and pieces of shrapnel splattered along the fuselage. One piece came into the cockpit and got me in the arm. There was bags of blood. My airspeed indicator had been shot away. I lost a lot of blood, so I turned on the oxygen again so as to keep conscious. I made an emergency landing and wandered around until I linked up with the Commandos. They patched me up and I staggered back to Malta the next day.'

The same journalist also described No 92 Sqn's CO, Sqn Ldr P H Humphreys, who had two and one shared victories to his name;

'A veteran of both the Battle of Britain and the war in the Mediterranean at the age of just 23. Husky, blonde, sensible and fearless – a born leader. He had a real sense of humour – but grim.'

Another ace to fall on 10 July was Flt Lt Raoul Daddo-Langlois of No 93 Sqn, who was heard over the radio to say that he 'had got one'. Moments later his Spitfire was also hit by friendly anti-aircraft fire and he crash-landed on a beach, sustaining a serious head injury. As Daddo-Langlois was being taken out to a hospital ship off shore, the lighter he was on was sunk in another raid and the young ace was lost. He was avenged in part by the squadron's future New Zealand ace Flg Off Stan Browne, who shot down a Ju 88 for his third victory.

The busy day brought success for other aces too, one being No 242 Sqn's CO, Sqn Ldr Mike Boddington, who, during the morning, shot down an He 111 from I./KG 26 that was attempting to attack shipping. His No 2, Flg Off Colin Coulthard, noted in his logbook;

'Dawn cover to invasion. Squadron two destroyed and two damaged. CO a Ju 88, and later CO and self bounced eight '109s and CO disintegrated one. Snell missing.'

Also flying with No 242 Sqn as supernumeraries on 10 July were SAAF aces Lt Col Laurie Wilmot and Maj Charles Laubscher.

The beachheads were soon secured and extended so that by nightfall the Pachino peninsula was in Allied hands, Syracuse had fallen and Licata had been captured by the Americans.

Sqn Ldr Boddington was successful again the next day when, flying southeast of Gela shortly after 0630 hrs, he sighted a Ju 88 that he attacked. He saw its port engine catch fire and large pieces fly off before the aircraft was finished off by Flg Off J A Stock. Unteroffizier Oskar Klammer's burning Ju 88D 'F6+NK' from 2.(F)/122 crashed into a wooded valley.

Later that same morning, shortly before 1100 hrs, No 72 Sqn's Sqn Ldr 'Dan' Daniel led a patrol near Syracuse and intercepted a formation

The suntanned pilots of No 242 Sqn pose for a photograph on Malta shortly before moving to Sicily on 22 July 1943. This group boasted several aces within its ranks, including the CO, Sqn Ldr Mike Boddington, who is seated in the centre of the front row wearing the forage cap (*C W Coulthard*)

of Italian fighters. The ace duly shared in the destruction of an 'MC 200' (his victim was actually a Fiat G.50) with Flt Lt M V Christopherson. Flg Off George Keith shot down another G.50, as well as a Ju 88, to become the squadron's latest ace. However, during the course of the action he had become detached from the rest of the squadron, and upon running short of fuel he force-landed within the beachhead at Pachino.

No 244 Wing Leader Wg Cdr Peter Olver, flying with No 92 Sqn, was also in the thick of the action on 11 July;

'We saw a formation of about a dozen Ju 88s coming towards the Americans. They did too steep a turn to port when they saw our Spitfires, which threw their formation into disarray before they reached the target. I took the last '88 and it went down below the remainder, which were scrambling back into a bunch and retiring up north. The other Spits took on other '88s. My Ju crashed after the crew bailed out. My own aircraft must have got a stray bullet in the fuel tank.'

Force-landing his personal aircraft (EN448/PO), Olver, who sustained some burns and wounds, was captured. He was replaced as the No 244 Wing Leader by another successful ace, Wg Cdr Wilf Duncan-Smith. The rest of No 92 Sqn chased the retreating bombers, claiming four more shot down, including one to Milt Jowsey – this was his third kill, and he eventually became an ace in late 1944 whilst serving with No 442 Sqn. Also claiming a Ju 88 was future ace Flg Off Stan Browne, who shared the kill with fellow No 93 Sqn Kiwi Plt Off Roy Fisher.

No 93 Sqn had intercepted a formation of bombers attacking ships waiting to off-load. Browne's Spitfire was then mistaken for an enemy aircraft by HMS *Warspite* and was hit by the battleship's anti-aircraft fire. Browne force-landed at Pachino, so becoming one of the first pilots to land in Sicily, although not quite in the manner he had expected! Finally, during the evening No 111 Sqn also had some success when its CO, George Hill, downed one of three Re.2002s credited to his unit, although he had identified his radial-engined victim as an Fw 190.

MOVE TO SICILY

The next day, 12 July, Ponte Olivo landing ground was captured and the Spitfire wings made preparations to move across from Malta. No 72 Sqn's Flg Off George Keith's earlier experiences did not deter him as during an early patrol on this date he was credited with another victory over the Syracuse-Augusta area. Towards midday the squadron's Flg Off Tom Hughes led a formation of eight to the Syracuse area, where they became hotly engaged with enemy fighters that were apparently escorting a Ju 52/3m that promptly became the first of eight victories for Plt Off Bruce Ingalls. Hughes then described the action against the escort;

'Opening up, I gained a little height and the bandits started to dive northwards. They appeared to be the slow but very manoeuvrable Macchi 200 (again, they were G.50s) of the *Regia Aeronautica*. My friends were in line abreast, having good shooting practice above me. Suddenly, the Italians broke formation. An amazing wheeling melee followed. Cameron, the Canadian, was turning tightly with an aerobatic "Wop". I joined him, and within two turns I was right on the fighter's tail. A one second burst from my cannons set him ablaze. It was fearful to see, but there was a parachute near Melilli, so I think the pilot got out.'

Also involved was his CO, 'Dan' Daniel, who shot down a Bf 109 for his 12th victory. In total, No 72 Sqn claimed six enemy fighters.

Later that day No 601 Sqn's CO, Sqn Ldr John Taylor, led eight Spitfires that intercepted a formation of Italian Ju 87Ds from 237ª *Squadriglia*, led by Maggiore Orlandini, over the port of Augusta. Minutes earlier the Stukas had successfully attacked Allied shipping. Taylor shot down the Ju 87 flown by Tenente Marcocci to claim his 14th victory, all of which had been achieved over North Africa and the Mediterranean, but return fire from the Stuka's gunner hit his aircraft. The 23-year-old ace initially attempted to bail out, but then headed towards Pachino to make a forced landing. However, Taylor was killed when his fighter crashed near Syracuse. He was replaced as CO of No 601 Sqn by the famous Polish ace Sqn Ldr Stanislaw Skalski.

13 July proved to be the last day on which the Luftwaffe appeared in strength over Sicily, and its efforts to stop the Allied advance westwards from Syracuse were to meet with failure. Augusta was occupied in the early hours of the 13th, with its crucial port installations almost intact, while the airfield at Pachino, which had been ploughed up by the Germans, was also made ready for use.

An early success was claimed by Sqn Ldr Hill of No 111 Sqn when, shortly after 0500 hrs, a dozen Spitfires that he was leading over the landing beaches intercepted six Ju 88s from II./KG 1 off Augusta. Two were downed, one by the CO and the other by future Australian ace Flt Lt Laurie McIntosh – Hill would destroy an Fw 190 three hours later. Sqn Ldr 'Rosie' Mackie's No 243 Sqn was also on patrol over the beaches, and it continued a remarkable run of success when 12 Spitfires flying over 'Acid' beach spotted an equal number of unescorted Italian Ju 87s south of Gerbini. Five of the dive-bombers were shot down, two by Mackie;

'We attacked from astern, having come out of the sun. I made attacks on three enemy aircraft. I attacked one Ju 87 from astern, firing from a range of 100 yards, and giving it another short burst from a distance of 60 yards. Its bomb was jettisoned. The Ju 87 disintegrated in mid air. I attacked another from astern at 50 yards. This aircraft burst into flames.'

At about the same time, No 93 Sqn, led by 'Sheep' Gilroy, was patrolling the Augusta area when enemy fighters were spotted. Amongst those to claim was Sgt Jim Andrew, who brought down a Bf 109, as described by a colleague who was in trouble;

'Luckily, Sgt Andrew had climbed into the sun and attacked the rearmost '109, leaving it in flames. This manoeuvre certainly discouraged the remaining '109s that were on my tail.'

Andrew also shot down a troop-carrying He 111 to set himself on the path to acedom.

After his forced landing two days earlier, Flg Off Stan Browne of No 72 Sqn was back in action, engaging some more Bf 109Gs;

'Pat Rivett and I attacked a Messerschmitt over Sicily and drove it down. We chased it into a valley and it was unable to turn left or right. We were getting closer to it but the pilot was so busy evading us that he hit the ground, tumbling over. Neither of us had fired a shot.'

Notwithstanding the unusual means of destruction, Leutnant Josef Dritthuber's demise elevated the New Zealander to ace status.

The rough state of the Sicilian airstrips is readily apparent as this well-armed groundcrew prepare to get No 43 Sqn Spitfire VC ES353/FT-Y ready for a sortie at Comiso on 21 July 1943 (*Official via J D R Rawlings*)

Future ace Flt Lt Cyril Bamberger was also successful, shooting down a lone Stuka that he encountered south of Catania for his fourth victory – and only one with No 93 Sqn.

In a later sortie, No 324 Wing Leader Wg Cdr Hugh 'Cocky' Dundas and Sqn Ldr Evan Mackie each claimed an Re.2002 of 5° *Stormo Assalto* destroyed, these aircraft being intercepted whilst dive-bombing warships off Augusta. Around the same time No 93 Sqn's CO, Sqn Ldr Wilf Sizer, claimed his 12th, and final, success when he downed a C.202 near Augusta. He was also credited with a C.202 probable and four more Macchi fighters damaged in an eventful combat.

During the afternoon of this hectic day, the first Spitfire squadrons of the Desert Air Force (DAF) flew in from Malta when No 244 Wing (Nos 1 SAAF, 92, 145, 417 and 601 Sqns) moved in to Pachino, as Wg Cdr Duncan-Smith noted. 'Thus 244 earned the distinction of being the first RAF formation to operate again from Continental soil since the fall of France in 1940'. The wing quickly settled in, and during the next three days more RAF Spitfire squadrons were transferred to Comiso.

One of the first patrols over the beaches on the 14th was by No 72 Sqn, and at 0745 hrs its pilots claimed three Bf 109Gs of I./JG 77 near Augusta. Amongst the victors was George Keith, who claimed his last 1.5 kills – the shared claim was made with fellow ace Plt Off Jack Hussey. The unit's third victory fell to Flg Off Ken Smith. Elsewhere, No 92 Sqn had a brush with some Italian C.202s, Milt Jowsey claiming one, and No 1 Sqn SAAF again fell victim to poor recognition by USAAF fighters as ace Lt 'Robbie' Robinson recounted to journalist Richard McMillan;

'I was five miles east of Catania at 10,000 ft when I was attacked. My Spit turned over on her side. She must have been hit in the engine, which cut. Oil sprayed over the windscreen and came into the cockpit. The cockpit began to fill with white smoke. I gave her the normal corrective, giving her opposite stick, until I got her straight and level. Then she began shuddering like a leaf. I kept on the lookout for further attacks, but none developed. One of our Spits was covering me from behind. He never came in again.

'I had the choice of ditching or bailing out. The Spit is not the type to ditch. I got ready to bail out. I opened the cockpit door, pulled the earpieces out of the helmet, ripped off my oxygen mask and started to roll. The next thing I knew I was tumbling into space.'

He safely got into his dinghy and was rescued by a Greek destroyer.

Enemy air power in Sicily was by now broken, and on 15 July, Spitfires flew 171 sorties on offensive patrols over the Catania and Gerbini areas and not one enemy machine was seen. The DAF's fighter wings had effectively driven the Luftwaffe from Sicilian skies, although there were still daily encounters, but on a much smaller scale. Plt Off Alan Peart had cause to remember one such encounter on 16 July when he had a narrow escape, and witnessed some stunning shooting by his Rhodesian colleague, and fellow ace, Flg Off William Maguire;

'Suddenly, a '109 appeared right by my wingtip. He'd made the perfect "bounce", and I should have been dead. I felt as if I was part of a film. I distinctly remember the pilot wearing his oxygen mask, glaring at me through the cockpit. He then pulled back on the stick and climbed out of range. Maguire also pulled up and took a 90-degree deflection shot, catching the '109 fair in the cockpit. It was a wonderful shot, and the German pilot did not survive his attack on me.'

Over Catania a No 232 Sqn patrol was bounced by about 15 Bf 109s from II. and III./JG 27 out of the sun. In the ensuing fight several Messerschmitts were hit and two shot down, one by Plt Off Joe Ekbery for his third victory.

The British and Canadian beachheads extended still further on 17 July, whilst above them the air action continued. One of the first engagements involved No 154 Sqn, which intercepted a mixed formation of Bf 109s and C.202s. A Macchi fell to Flt Lt Alan Aikman, giving him his tenth, and final, success. No 81 Sqn was still flying from Malta at this point, and the following afternoon the unit's Flg Off Bill Maguire claimed his eighth victory when he shot down an Fw 190. Then, during a morning patrol over a convoy on the 19th, No 152 Sqn's Flg Off Norman Jones made a significant start on the road to acedom when, during a patrol to the south of Augusta, he destroyed three Re.2002s of 5° *Stormo Assalto* as they attempted to attack Allied shipping. Three more

Plt Off Alan Peart served with No 81 Sqn in North Africa, during the invasion of Sicily and in Italy, before moving with the unit to Burma in late 1943. There, he achieved acedom to become one of the few pilots to claim victories over the Germans, Italians and Japanese (*A M Peart*)

In order to spread the improved capabilities offered by the Spitfire IX amongst as many units as possible, No 81 Sqn handed some of its aircraft over to other units, receiving Mk VCs in their stead. On 16 July Plt Off Alan Peart was flying this machine, JK322/FL-4, over Catania when he damaged a Bf 109. It is seen a month later following a German night raid on Lentini (*A M Peart*)

No 152 Sqn's Spitfire VC LZ807/UM-V is refuelled at Lentini East on 5 August 1943. Eleven days earlier, on 25 July, Sgt Len Smith had used it to shoot down a Ju 52/3m for his fourth victory – it was one of eight claimed by the squadron in the action. He moved with No 152 Sqn to Burma later in the year, where he became an ace in 1944 (*C W Coulthard*)

During the Sicily campaign Wg Cdr Colin Gray (second from right) was the leader of No 322 Wing, and thus had the privilege of adorning his aircraft with his initials. At Lentini in late July, his mount was Spitfire IX MA408, which he used until he became tour expired in September (*C F Gray*)

Reggianes were shot down by his squadronmates, including one by another future ace, Sgt Len Smith, who also shared a second.

Soon after No 152 Sqn's success No 1 Sqn SAAF, led by Capt Hannes Faure, was directed onto a trio of Fw 190s. Faure shared in the destruction of one of them with Lt van der Merwe, thus taking his final tally to six destroyed. Faure's victory was also the squadron's first over Europe. He was made CO of the unit soon afterwards.

More units were now moving to airfields in Sicily, and by 25 July most Axis aircraft had been evacuated from the island. Patrols from the mainland continued, however, and some C.202s remained on Sicily.

With its fighters defeated in the air, the Luftwaffe's transport units did what they could by flying in reinforcements, fuel and ammunition, albeit once again at great cost. The Ju 52/3m supply trains were known to be landing on the beaches near Milazzo, and on 25 July 33 Spitfires from Wg Cdr Colin Gray's No 322 Wing encountered a 'gaggle' of Junkers transports preparing to land on an improvised strip in this area. Gray led his pilots into attack before the escorting Bf 109s could intervene, and within a few minutes a dozen transports had been shot down. Loaded with petrol, they exploded in spectacular fashion, and many of the Spitfires were hit by fragments. The German fighters dived on Gray's wing, but they were held off. The slaughter then continued until 21 of the Ju 52/3ms had crashed into the sea or along the beaches, together with four escorts. It had been a 'red letter' day, with Gray claiming two;

'I saw three Junkers in formation just ahead of me, and a shot at the leader caused him to burst into flames and dive into the sea. I then turned to his No 2, and the same thing happened. From the spectacular results it looked as if the transports must have been carrying petrol. It was all over in a few seconds.'

These were Gray's final victories. With 27 and one shared destroyed and a further 22 probably destroyed or damaged, he was the most successful New Zealand pilot of the war.

No 152 Sqn was also in the thick of the action, claiming eight transports and a brace of fighters, No 242 Sqn downed seven transports and two fighters and No 81 Sqn's score was four Ju 52/3ms and a trio of Bf 109s destroyed. Among the successful pilots was Norman Jones of No 152 Sqn, who, having made his first three victory claims just four days earlier, shared in the destruction of one of the transports and then shot down two of the escorting Bf 109s. The pilot of the second fighter bailed out just as Jones opened fire!

Also successful with one and one shared Ju 52/3ms destroyed was squadronmate Flt Lt Geoff Baynham, who said that he was so close to one of his victims when it blew up that his cockpit was filled with smoke. After landing he discovered a length of parachute cord trapped in his radiator. His colleague, Sgt Len Smith, also shot down one of the transports for his fourth success. He later became an ace over Burma. Among No 242 Sqn's claimants was Flt Sgt Eric Doherty, who shot down three Ju 52/3ms to start him on his path to 'acedom'. In No 81 Sqn, Sgt Don Rathwell also claimed a tri-motor, while Flt Sgt Larry Cronin shot down two Bf 109Gs for the first of his five victories. Their CO, ace Sqn Ldr 'Babe' Whitamore, also added another to his score. Despite some inevitable overclaiming, the Spitfire units had enjoyed a stunning success.

The presence of Spitfire IXs over Sicily had not gone unnoticed, as Major Johannes Steinhoff, *Kommodore* of JG 77, wrote;

'The Malta Spitfires are back again. They're fitted with a high altitude supercharger, and at anything over 25,000 ft they just play cat and mouse with us.'

It was in one of them soon afterwards that No 92 Sqn's Rhodesian ace Flg Off 'Dicky' Dicks-Sherwood gained revenge for his recent wounding when he shot down lone Bf 109G Wk-Nr 18119 'White 5' of 1./JG 77, flown by Unteroffizier Karl-Eugen Hettler, who bailed out into the sea and became a PoW. He was the Rhodesian's eighth, and final, victim.

When the squadrons moved into the captured airfields, they sometimes yielded a 'prize'. No 72 Sqn acquired a Saiman 200 biplane trainer, whilst Wg Cdr Colin Gray flew a captured C.202 commenting;

'It was very manoeuvrable, but certainly inferior in performance to the Spitfire IX. It was probably better than the Spitfire Vs that we still had in Sicily, however.'

With the skies more secure, ground strafing now began to feature, with 8.5-victory ace Flg Off George Keith of No 72 Sqn succumbing to ground fire on 4 August. Catania fell to the 8th Army the very next day, and the enemy began evacuating across the Strait of Messina to the Italian mainland. On the 7th another New Zealander Flt Lt Leighton Montgomerie of No 81 Sqn began his path to ace status when, during an escort mission for USAAF P-40s over the Strait of Messina, he spotted a low-flying aircraft. Descending, he and his section intercepted a Caproni Ca.309 Ghibli light transport aircraft and shot it down.

Despite relentless Allied air attacks, during the night of 16 August the last German troops were evacuated from Sicily. The following day saw the entry of the 8th Army into Messina, and this effectively brought an

Kommodore of JG 77 over Sicily in 1943 was one of the Luftwaffe's leading *experten*, Maj Johannes 'Macki' Steinhoff, who wrote tellingly of the Spitfire IXs at the time 'they just play cat and mouse with us' (*Robert Forsyth*)

One of the outstanding individual combats of the Sicily campaign was flown by Flt Sgt Eric Doherty of No 242 Sqn, who is seen here nonchalantly leaning on the barrel of his 20 mm cannon. On 25 July he shot down three Ju 52/3ms off Cap Rascolm to claim his first kills. He was to achieve four more over Italy the following year (*C W Coulthard*)

end to the Sicilian campaign. One of the last combats came on 28 August when No 81 Sqn, led by new No 322 Wing Leader SAAF ace Lt Col Laurie Wilmot, was escorting Bostons to bomb a railway junction in southern Italy. Six Bf 109s (led by 20-victory *experte* Oberfeldwebel Rudolf Taschnerhom) of I./JG 53 attacked, but Flt Sgt Win Robinson of No 81 Sqn shot two of them down. Simultaneously, Wilmot engaged and shot down another Messerschmitt to thus become the last ace of the Sicilian campaign. A fourth Bf 109 was claimed by Alan Peart for his third victory, and he recalled the action specially for this volume;

'We had frequent clashes with enemy fighters over the Strait of Messina when escorting our bombers, and on this occasion we were attacked by Me 109s over the sea. In the ensuing melee, after shooting down one, I found that I had latched onto a really experienced German pilot. He knew all the tricks, and after sparring around for a while trying to get on each other's tail, we, by mutual consent, broke it off to look for easier prey. This was the aircraft that Robinson forced into the ground.

'My logbook records that I was in Spitfire IX FL-J, and six Me 109s bounced our section without result. Chased one for ten minutes all over the sky. He finally crashed just inside the coast.

'Our task on that occasion was escorting bombers over the Gulf of Eupherme. Don't ask me where that is now, as I have no idea!'

Early the following morning Wg Cdr Wilf Duncan-Smith led a dawn patrol that spotted some Fw 190s as they dived into cloud;

'I chased after the enemy and was immediately shot at by a second Fw 190, which dived in over my left shoulder. Tracers streaked past my port wing, and it shot past very close. The pilot unwisely straightened up, giving me an excellent opportunity to open fire on him from slightly below on a fine quarter. I saw strikes on his wing root and the bottom of the cockpit, and with smoke trailing he disappeared into a thick cloud.'

His 17th victory was over Leutnant Bruno Schäfer of 9./SKG 10, and the latter's demise was just about the last aerial action over Sicily.

Operations now began in preparation for the next phase – the Allied landings in Italy and a return to mainland Europe.

Sicilian airfields provided a rich crop of enemy aircraft that were captured in a flyable state, and many units had a 'hack' adorned with their codes. No 92 Sqn, for example, acquired this Arado Ar 66c trainer. Ace Flg Off Milt Jowsey and Plt Off Rex Probert are posing with the biplane (*via B Cull*)

ITALY – THE LONG FLOG

The invasion of Italy commenced on 3 September when British forces began crossing the Strait of Messina to land at Reggio Calabria on the 'toe' of Italy. They did so under massive air cover, with the experiences of No 92 Sqn being typical. Its aircraft took off before dawn and maintained a standing patrol over the Strait throughout the day. Fw 190 fighter-bombers were intercepted on two occasions, and they were forced to jettison their bombs and withdraw.

Spitfires from No 1 Sqn SAAF were also up, and Lt Douglas Hastie had an exciting day when, in the vicinity of Reggio, he damaged a C.202, but his aircraft was also hit and a loss of coolant eventually caused it to catch fire. Hastie bailed out moments later. A patrol from No 111 Sqn went one better the next day when a flight led by Flg Off 'Hap' Kennedy intercepted several Fw 190s carrying bombs as they dived onto some destroyers. Kennedy managed to damage one, after which he chased it all the way to Cape Vaticano. Presumably thinking that he was safe, Oberfeldwebel Josef Kern of III./SKG 10 reduced his speed, at which point Kennedy shot the Fw 190 into the sea to claim his ninth victory.

The following day No 154 Sqn's recently appointed flight commander, Rhodesian William Maguire, claimed the first of his six victories with the unit when he shot down Do 217K-2 '6N+CD' of *Stab*/KG 100 south of Naples. He also claimed three fighters destroyed before the month was out.

The landings had an immediate effect in that Italian forces unconditionally surrendered on 8 September. This did little to reduce the fighting, however, as the Germans and Fascist Italians continued to fiercely oppose the Allied advance. On the 9th British and American troops carried out a major amphibious assault at Salerno, to the south

Flying from Lentini, No 152 Sqn covered the crossing of the Strait of Messina and also the landings at Salerno in early September 1943. Flt Lt 'Macielk' Dreki was flying Spitfire VC MA289/UM-T over the Italian mainland on the 11th of the month when he shot down a Bf 109 for his his fourth victory. His promising career was cut short two days later, however, when he was killed in a collision with another Spitfire (*T Dreki via W Matusiak*)

of Naples, and once again the Spitfire units covered the landings. Amongst others, No 1 Sqn SAAF was over 'Peaches' beach early, although shortly afterwards it left No 244 Wing and joined the all South African No 7 SAAF Wing.

There was considerable action over Salerno on the 10th, and one of those to lodge victory claims was 'Hap' Kennedy in a Spitfire IX. He managed to get another Fw 190, whose demise he recalled drew a response from the formation leader, Gp Capt 'Sheep' Gilroy. 'Who shot down that aircraft? "Blue Three, Sir", I answered, not quite sure of what was coming. "Bloody good show! Let's go home chaps!"'

The landings also saw the enemy use a variety of new weapons, including *Fritz-X* and Hs 293 radio-guided bombs that on 13 September were used against the battleship *Warspite*. Flying above the vessel at the time, the Spitfire pilots saw the ship apparently struck by a torpedo, but the covering pilots from No 81 Sqn saw no sign of any torpedo-bombers below. They did, however, sight three Do 217s making their escape north up the coast. The Spitfires split up in order to attack the enemy bombers, but effective return fire sent a fighter down. One section destroyed a Dornier just prior to Plt Off Alan Peart leading his section in;

'I saw pieces come off its port wing, but could see no result from the others. My next attack caused a large piece to detach, and I flew right into it! There was a loud bang, but I seemed to be all right. The Dornier crash-landed on a scrub-covered hillside. I flew over the downed aircraft, and although I could see no sign of life, the crew probably did survive. I felt it was a fine effort by these three Germans, and wished them luck to survive following such a brave and audacious attack.'

With his aircraft damaged, and all three aircraft in his section running out of fuel, Peart and his men landed on a rough strip within the beachhead. This proved to be Alan Peart's final victory in the Mediterranean, and he later became an ace following No 81 Sqn's move to Burma, so becoming one of that select band of pilots to claim victories over German, Italian and Japanese aircraft.

Action continued over the beachhead as the enemy threw in air attacks against the invaders, and there were regular clashes. Having left No 145 Sqn's Polish Fighting Team after the Tunisian campaign, Flt Lt Eugeniusz Horbaczewski joined No 43 Sqn. In good weather in the early afternoon of the 16th, he was over the Salerno beaches and was about to end his patrol when a dozen Fw 190s were spotted below them diving away to the east;

'We chased enemy aircraft for about three minutes and I closed on one of them to 200 yards at about 300 ft. I gave Fw 190 two short bursts of "mixed" fire, and I saw strikes. After second burst enemy aircraft half-rolled and went straight down and hit the deck about three miles southeast of Campagna. I started to chase two more Fw 190s and opened fire on the port one from about 250 yards range at deck level, with starboard cannon only, giving a number of short bursts finishing all ammo. As a result of this fire enemy aircraft caught fire in portside of engine and I saw strikes in cockpit area. Enemy aircraft went down and crashed ten miles northeast of Campagna.'

The legendary 'Dziubek's' only victories with No 43 Sqn had taken his tally to 11 kills.

During the Salerno landings the Luftwaffe used guided bombs in attacks on Allied shipping, with some success. On 20 September Flg Off Roy Hussey of No 72 Sqn shot down two Do 217M missile carriers, the crew of the second one bailing out, as can be seen from this remarkable image taken from his gun camera film (*R D Scrase*)

Following the Italian surrender the Free French moved quickly to reoccupy the island of Corsica, the liberating force including two Spitfire *Groupes des Chasse*. A number of successful pilots served with these units, including Cdt Henri Hugo (CO of GC II/7), who is seen here, somewhat bizarrely, in swimming trunks briefing two of his pilots in front of ER863 at Campo dell'Oro, near Ajaccio (*ECPA*)

Despite KG 100 suffering steady losses they continued to attack Allied ships, and on the 20th it was No 72 Sqn that had a successful day. Plt Off Roy Hussey's wingman recalled;

'We were at about 20,000 ft and heading towards two Do 217s. At that moment I had trouble with my second-stage supercharger, which kept cutting in and out. Roy flew on ahead and shot down the first Dornier. By the time I had sorted out my problems, he had caught up with the second aircraft and got that one too. As I came up alongside him the crew were bailing out, but the last, who was in too much of a hurry to pull his ripcord, went down with his aeroplane, the parachute see-sawing up and down the tailplane.'

Despite the fighters' best efforts, over the next few days the Do 217s carrying Hs 293 guided bombs inflicted considerable damage on Allied shipping. Also claiming at this time was No 152 Sqn's Kiwi CO, 21-year-old Sqn Ldr Bruce Ingram, who downed an Fw 190 on the 19th and shared another three days later, which was his 14th, and final, victory. Like many other units, No 152 Sqn was by now based in Italy, and remained so until November when it was sent with No 81 Sqn to Burma.

CORSICAN INTERLUDE

The sudden Italian surrender had left the garrison on Corsica in limbo, but the German force of 20,000+ men remained active. Fighting with local Corsican partisans soon broke out, and the French government in exile quickly requested that the island be re-occupied. Spitfire-equipped GCs I/3 and II/7 were ordered to support the French forces that had landed to liberate the island, and they began flying across to Campo dell'Oro, near Ajaccio, on 24 September.

That day the German evacuation was covered by Fw 190s from II./SG 2, three of which attacked the destroyer *Fantasque*. Sous-Lt Michel Gruyelle shot one down to claim the first victory for the French Spitfires over Corsica. They were replaced on patrol by Cne Henri Hugo and Sgt Chef Henri Planchard, and although the latter was downed in a furious fight with more Fw 190s, he was credited with a Focke-Wulf destroyed.

With the arrival of the ground party by sea, both units quickly became established on French soil and began attacks on the shipping evacuating the Germans.

Over the sea off Ghissonaccia on the 29th, Cne Roger Duval spotted some Ar 196 floatplanes of SAGr 128, one of which was shot down in flames and a second apparently stalled into the sea when evading. When chasing the remaining pair, the Spitfires spotted a formation of seven Ju 52/3ms. They made three

head-on passes at them and shot four transports down. On returning to Campo dell'Oro Duval, Adj Chef Marcel Martin, Cne Prayer and Sgt Chef Jean Sarrail were each credited with a Ju 52/3m. Additionally, Prayer, Sarrail and Lt Felix Brunct each downed a floatplane. GC I/3 ace Cne Roger Duval was also credited with a Ju 52/3m for his final victory.

A few hours later Cdt Henry Hoarau de La Source and Lt Henri Jeandet were scrambled after a Ju 88 that had appeared over Ajaccio, and they shot it down in flames. It was the harbinger of an incoming raid, and four more Spitfires led by Cne Gabrielle Gauthier took off and joined up with the original pair. They were vectored onto a formation of Do 217Es from II./KG 100, while four other Spitfires returning from a mission to Bastia also headed towards them, at which point the enemy formation broke up. Three of the bombers evaded the fighters and released weapons, as Henri Jeandet described;

'Unfortunately, the first three Dorniers that got past us succeeded in getting within range of their targets – the ships at anchor. I was a long way off, but went after them with the throttle wide open. To my great surprise, bright points of light dropped away from the three bombers and shot several hundred yards ahead of them towards the harbour then exploded, destroying a British transport ship and almost hitting a French torpedo boat.'

He had witnessed the launching of Hs 293 rocket-propelled and radio-guided bombs. However, KG 100's nemesis then arrived, and in the next few minutes the French Spitfires claimed six of the Do 217s destroyed. Future ace Gauthier was credited with one of them off Cap Sette Nave, whilst Lt Georges Valentin who had become an ace during 1940, was also credited with a Dornier destroyed. The two Do 217s shared by Henri Jeandet took him to acedom – the first French pilot to achieve this distinction whilst flying Spitfires in the Mediterranean.

There was further action over Corsica the next day too when shortly before lunch two sections off the northwest coast spotted a pair of six-engined Me 323s, and each was attacked by one flight. The first one – thought to have been Wk-Nr 1216 'DT+1P' of II./TG 5 – exploded

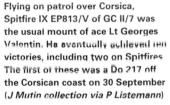

Flying on patrol over Corsica, Spitfire IX EP813/V of GC II/7 was the usual mount of ace Lt Georges Valentin. He eventually achieved ten victories, including two on Spitfires. The first of these was a Do 217 off the Corsican coast on 30 September (*J Mutin collection via P Listemann*)

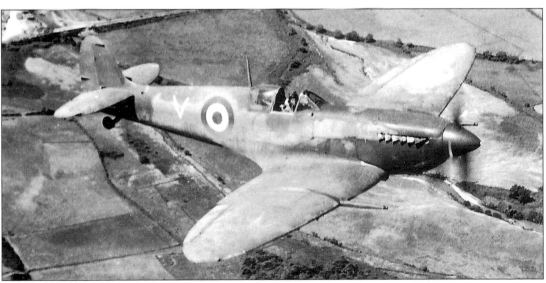

under the fire of Lt Georges Blanck and Sgt Albert Causse – Blanck's only Spitfire victory was his 12th, and last, kill. The other section of Lts Georges Pissotte and Jaquet and Sous-Lt Verrier chased the remaining Me 323, which stubbornly refused to go down. However, finding himself alone, Marcel Verrier eventually finished the job and the huge transport crashed onto a beach. They then had to turn to face a new threat, as six Bf 109s dived on them. Although neither side caused any damage, Georges Blanck was almost hit by the jettisoned drop tank of one of the Messerschmitts! Verrier had, meanwhile, been forced to bail out, and he was picked up by the Germans. Managing to escape, he returned to his unit a few days later after several adventures.

On 3 October GCs I/3 and II/7 became part of 1ere *Escadre de Chasse* – or No 332 (Free French) Wing in RAF parlance – under Cdt Marie Papin-Labazordiere. The following day Operation *Vesuvius*, the reoccupation of Corsica, ended. It was the first French territory to be liberated from the Germans, though the latter had managed to evacuate 20,000+ men, albeit with severe losses to their air transport force.

There continued to be occasional brushes with the Luftwaffe off the island, such as on 30 October when a Ju 88 was shot down by several pilots, the shared victory elevating Cne Gabriel Gauthier to ace status.

ACES' AUTUMN

By now the superb Spitfire VIII, considered by many pilots as the finest of all the Spitfire variants, was being delivered in some numbers. On 2 October SAAF ace Capt Bennie Osler, who was a flight commander with No 145 Sqn, made his first flight in a Mk VIII, and west of Termoli shared in the destruction of Oberfeldwebel Peter Pellander's Fw 190. Osler assumed command of No 601 Sqn soon afterwards. No 417 Sqn also had Spitfire VIIIs, and two days later RCAF ace Flt Lt Bert Houle led a section that included future aces Flg Off Don Gordon and Sgt Jack Doyle on a patrol over the Italian east coast. With Termoli now in British hands, trouble was expected, and bomb bursts soon announced the presence of enemy aircraft. Houle, leading his section in a dive on the intruders – identified as Fw 190s – recounted in his report;

'I was the only one successful in dropping my long-range tank. Diving to about 1000 ft, I saw a Fw 190 above me, going northwestwards. I pulled up and got two short bursts from about 200-250 yards. On the second burst I saw an explosion on the Fw 190's tail or rear fuselage. It then went vertically down into cloud at 2000 ft.'

Moments later Houle damaged another fighter and then went after a third, ruefully noting 'I chased him up the Sangro Valley, right on the deck, hedge-hopping all the way. I should have got him, but didn't'. However, he had claimed No 417 Sqn's first victory since Sicily, and enthused, 'I found out for certain that the Spitfire VIII could certainly catch an Fw 190. My favourite fighter was the Spitfire VIII with clipped wings. It had power and good armament. It could roll quickly and out-turn any enemy fighter we encountered'.

Although Italy had been knocked out of the war, the Germans were still determined to hold their ground, and the rugged terrain was ideal for defence. There would be no swift victory in Italy for the Allies. The Luftwaffe was also putting much effort into slowing the Allied advance, and Fw 190 fighter-bombers of SKG 10 were regularly encountered. Sqn Ldr 'Rosie' Mackie was leading a mixed formation of No 243 Sqn Spitfire Vs and IXs between Salerno and Naples on 11 October when hostile aircraft were reported and bomb bursts seen, but they could not catch the bombers;

'When flying southwards to resume our patrol, I noticed another bomb burst near the southern end of the beach and observed a Do 217 at 16,000 ft – 3000 ft above us – turning to port, and making off north-northwest. I climbed after the enemy aircraft, which then dived. I fired two bursts but saw no results, and broke as enemy fighters were reported behind us. The enemy aircraft went into cloud and I followed. During the chase in and out of cloud I fired several bursts, experiencing return fire from the enemy aircraft. After seeing strikes along the fuselage, I saw pieces break away. The enemy aircraft went down in a spiral dive and crashed, bursting into flames.'

It was Mackie's 14th victory.

Two days later No 93 Sqn, which had recently come under command of another Kiwi ace, Sqn Ldr Derek Westenra, found action when supporting the assault by the US 5th Army across the Volturno River in the face of fierce opposition on the land and in the air. All Spitfire squadrons flew cover to protect the bridgehead, and 'Hap' Kennedy, who was now a flight commander in No 93 Sqn engaged a Bf 109 that rolled and dived away from him. Kennedy, who was flying a Spitfire VC, soon caught him, and the unfortunate German did not survive the low-level bail out. On climbing up, Kennedy and his wingman were bounced by 12+ Messerschmitt fighters of III./JG 77, probably flown by 'tyros'. Eventually, Kennedy manoeuvred behind and below them and, despite only his port cannon firing, shot down the 'tail end Charlie'. He destroyed another Bf 109G on 15 October.

Most units were seeing action at this time, including No 232 Sqn, which in mid-October had moved into Gioia del Colle, on the east coast of Italy. On the 23rd Flt Lt W A Olmstead and Sgt L J Bowring were scrambled, and each destroyed a Bf 109G in the Bari area.

By now Allied forces had moved up to the formidable defences of the *Gustav* Line, which had the old monastery at Monte Cassino at its heart. The latter would be the scene of much bitter fighting through into the spring of 1944.

Seen between sorties at Tortorella, near Foggia, in October 1943, Spitfire IX EN459/HN-D of No 93 Sqn was used by Flt Lt 'Hap' Kennedy to bring down a Bf 109 at Sparanise on the 15th of that month. This was his 13th, and last, claim in the Mediterranean *(via W Matusiak)*

It was poor weather that claimed one of No 92 Sqn's aces when, on 28 October, Flt Sgt Michael Askey failed to return from a low-level sortie over the Adriatic Sea near Ancona. Soon afterwards his squadron gained a formidable new CO when 'Rosie' Mackie arrived. He was clearly pleased;

'My appointment as CO of No 92 Sqn, then based on the east coast of Italy, came on 5 November. As this was – then – the top-scoring fighter squadron in the RAF, I regarded it as something of an honour. It was flying Spitfire VIIIs, which were superior to any enemy aircraft we encountered in Italy, especially above 15,000 ft. Operations in this area were mainly patrols over the Sangro River, and there was considerable enemy aircraft activity.'

Another famous unit was also in action too when, over the frontlines on 6 November, No 43 Sqn's Flt Lt 'Paddy' Turkington claimed his fourth success when a pair of Bf 109s attacked him;

'I turned to meet this attack and started to tangle with one of the enemy aircraft. I got on his tail and the Me 109 did an aileron turn down to 1000 ft, when it pulled out I was astern and slightly below. He flew straight and level and I gave him a shot of my cannon, and I immediately saw strikes on the fuselage and noticed small pieces coming off. I closed to very short range, giving a long burst of cannon, with hits on the nose, and flames started to come from the engine. The enemy aircraft had now slowed down considerably, and it started going down towards the deck.'

Also successful was Flg Off Wilmer Reid, who destroyed another Messerschmitt near Venafro.

Across on the east coast at Foggia was No 417 Sqn, now led by Sqn Ldr Bert Houle, while just along the coast at Gioia del Colle was No 154 Sqn, in which Flt Lt William Maguire was a flight commander. Just after dawn on the 11th, he took off on a weather reconnaissance in Spitfire IX MA580/HT-S;

'North of the Volturno River mouth I sighted four Fw 190s travelling southwest from Isola at approximately 8000 ft. The section turned about and attacked from astern above, jettisoning overload tanks on the way down. I closed in to 200 yards on the rearmost enemy aircraft and fired two one-second bursts. There was a big flash on the cockpit, and enemy aircraft burst into flames and crashed slightly southeast of Sennine. Pieces kept coming off the fuselage all the way down.'

Maguire's last victory that made him one of the leading Rhodesian aces of the war is thought to have been over Unteroffizier Wilhelm Bulow of II./SG 4. Another ace who claimed his final victory at this time was No 111 Sqn's CO, Sqn Ldr Peter Matthews, who, on 2 December, shot down an Fi 156 near Pratola for his ninth victory – it was also his fifth in a Spitfire in the Mediterranean area. Unfortunately, he was injured in a road accident shortly afterwards and evacuated home.

The following day Bert Houle was over the Sangro River, and when en route home he spotted seven Bf 109s in a loose formation;

'Turning towards them, I gave one squirt on a deflection shot and pulled through, firing even after he had disappeared under the nose of my aircraft. When I straightened out, I was right behind another one, which I thought was the same aircraft. Out of the corner of my eye I noticed an aircraft plummeting for earth on fire and, at the same time, gave the '109 in front a good squirt up his jacksie from 200 to 250 yards, and directly from astern. The tail end immediately blew off with a blinding flash, a long streak of flames coming behind it, and the aircraft started to do slow rolls. Then, as the nose dropped, it went into a vertical spin and headed for the deck in flames. Bushe and myself both saw that the '109s crashed.'

'Rosie' Mackie, leading No 92 Sqn, also claimed a Bf 109 over the Sangro River that same day, as did other pilots in his squadron. Mackie claimed another (from I./JG 53) in the same area 48 hours later. And it was during an action on the 5th that one of his SAAF pilots, Lt Albert Sachs, won a DFC. The citation read;

'In December 1943 this officer was engaged on a patrol over the Sangro River when he sighted a large formation of fighter-bombers escorted by Messerschmitt 109s. He immediately led his section into the attack and, as a result, the bombers were forced to jettison their bombs. In the fight, Lt Sachs shot down one of the enemy aircraft. He also hit another one, causing it to explode in the air. His own aircraft was struck in the windscreen and mainplane by flying portions of the disintegrating aircraft. After this Lt Sachs was heavily engaged and his aircraft received such damage that it could no longer be flown, and he was forced to leave it by parachute. In this spirited action Lt Sachs displayed great courage and determination, and his example was worthy of the highest praise.'

The fighting over the Sangro River was tough, and on 8 December Bert Houle led his men into another fight that saw Flg Off Garth Horricks claim his penultimate victory – his first in a Spitfire. He then had to bail out, however, although he was picked up by some New Zealand soldiers and quickly returned to No 417 Sqn.

On the west coast, Cassino was the magnet for much action, and on the afternoon of 14 December No 43 Sqn was over the bomb line when it spotted some *Jabos*. One of the pilots engaged was Flg Off Reid;

'I went down on them. At a range of 2000 yards the two '190s broke east over a valley, climbing slightly. They mistakenly thought I was losing them, and they dived east into the main large valley. I chose the trailing '190 and closed quickly after they had dived. I gave him a long burst of machine gun fire from about 300 yards, pumping the control column to spray the '190. I observed strikes along the port side and black smoke came from port side of the engine. The enemy aircraft continued to fly straight and level. I went into line astern and gave it two short bursts of cannon and machine gun fire. The port tailplane buckled about two-thirds of the way from the tip and the '190 went straight into the deck.'

Wilmer Reid's final victory also made him the latest RCAF pilot to become an ace in this theatre. The increasingly bad weather then led to something of a respite for the rest of the year.

BLOODY ANZIO

The offensive against Cassino opened on 12 January 1944, and an amphibious landing was also planned on the west coast to the south of Rome so as to outflank the *Gustav* Line. In preparation for the landings several Spitfire squadrons, including Nos 92 and 93, moved coasts. However, it was at Foggia that the RAF's fighter force suffered a grievous loss when Wg Cdr Lance Wade, an ace with 24 victories, including ten on Spitfires, now of the DAF HQ Staff, was killed in a flying accident the same day that the First Battle of Cassino began. The latter was to end a month later in bloody stalemate.

The Allied invasion force approached the coast during the night of 21 January and troops began landing in the early hours of the following morning. Spitfires that had taken off in moonlight were over the beaches before dawn, and at first light pilots saw British and American troops coming ashore. By nightfall the ports at Anzio and Nettuno had been captured and the beachhead secured before the anticipated counter attack.

Maj Hannes Faure (left), CO of No 1 Sqn SAAF, congratulates Capt Vivian Voss, his adjutant, on his 50th birthday on 24 January 1944. Faure had 5.5 victories to his name while Voss had three – from flying Bristol F 2B Fighters with No 48 Sqn in World War 1! (*SAAF*)

Flt Sgt James Andrew (left) of No 93 Sqn is seen after his combat over Anzio on 27 January 1944, when he shot down two *Jabo* Bf 109s. His head is bandaged after he took a knock force-landing his Spitfire with engine failure. With Andrew is Capt Tom Taylor, who claimed a Messerschmitt in the same action. Andrew became an ace three weeks later, but was killed in Burma in 1945 (*No 607 Sqn Association*)

The whole operation, in fact, achieved complete surprise, largely thanks to Allied air superiority. Unfortunately, this opportunity was not exploited on the ground, resulting in much bitter fighting both in and over the area. Most squadrons were over the beachhead during the day, and they soon drew a response from the Luftwaffe. No 417 Sqn's CO, Bert Houle recalled;

'Soon, we noticed four aircraft flying a suspicious formation 6000 ft below, and as we started down to investigate I saw them releasing bombs. I ordered the boys to jettison their fuel tanks and dived to attack.

'I went after the rearmost of the four Fw 190s as it was turning inland for home. I had it lined up pretty well at less than 150 yards when I pressed the button. Immediately, large pieces fell off the underside of the fuselage, the left hand side of the engine and the top of the cockpit. Some of the oil from it spattered against my windscreen. Dense, black smoke poured from it. I was getting all set for another burst when everything seemed to hit my kite at once. There was a pattern of bullets on the armour plating behind me and, at the same time, I made a violent turn to starboard and up. I saw the enemy pass below, so whipped back and got a few bursts at him, without result.'

Houle's victim was probably Feldwebel Franz Juengels of I./JG 4. Two days later, having fought with No 72 Sqn since it first moved to North Africa, Flt Lt Roy Hussey claimed his final success when, over Anzio, he shared in the destruction of an Fw 190 to take his total to an impressive 14 victories, four of which were shared. He was rested soon afterwards. Houle's squadron remained regularly engaged, and he claimed another Bf 109 on 27 January during one of the many Luftwaffe fighter-bomber attacks on the Anzio beachhead.

No 93 Sqn was also engaged that day when Yorkshireman Flt Sgt James Andrew intercepted six bomb-carrying Bf 109s about to attack Allied shipping. In a brief fight he destroyed two. However, the engine on his aircraft then failed and he force-landed just behind the lines, sustaining a minor head injury. His colleague, Capt Tom Taylor, also shot down a Bf 109 and damaged another. This action was described in the citation for the award of the DFM to Andrew soon after he had become an ace;

'Early in 1944 Flt Sgt James Andrew, while on patrol over the Anzio beachhead, engaged two

Messerschmitts, shooting them down in quick succession. If the engine of his aircraft had not failed he would probably have destroyed a third hostile aircraft during this engagement. In all, he has downed five enemy aircraft. Throughout, this airman's great courage and determination in the face of the enemy has been an inspiring example to his fellow pilots.'

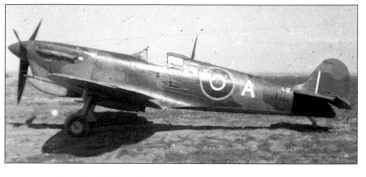

The dogged advance up the Adriatic coast continued, and from Canne at the end of January a new Spitfire unit began operations. No 274 Sqn, under desert ace Sqn Ldr John Morgan, mounted its first mission from Italy as the flight commander, Flt Lt Paddy Moon, recalled to the author;

'On the 24th we went on a strafe and recce of the Capestrano area, and with some "Kittybombers" attacked four tanks in the mountains, claiming three knocked out. We saw both heavy and light flak. From then on it was daily ground-attacking anything that moved. This was in support of the Anzio beachhead as the Germans, of course, were rushing support from the Adriatic side across the mountains.'

No 32 Sqn was also moved across the Mediterranean to Foggia, and the unit undertook its first operation on 2 February when the CO, Sqn Ldr M S Lewis, led his pilots in a sweep with No 73 Sqn.

It was over Anzio where the heaviest fighting remained, however, despite the often very indifferent weather. Amongst those who claimed was No 92 Sqn's Sqn Ldr 'Rosie' Mackie, who, off the coast on the 2nd, intercepted an Fw 190 as it levelled out over land, then closed in;

'I fired many short bursts and saw strikes on the fuselage just in front of the cockpit and starboard wing roots. Streams of white smoke trailed from the engine and there was a burst of flame. The '190 half rolled and, diving through cloud, crashed in a plume of dust.'

No 417 Sqn saw a fair bit of action too, with Sqn Ldr Houle bagging another Bf 109 on 7 February. One week later, over the beachhead, he shot down an Fw 190, as did Flg Off Garth Horricks. These were the

The badge and lightning bolt decorating Spitfire VC ER486/A announces that it is owned by No 274 Sqn. The unit began operations in Italy in the ground attack role in early 1944 when led by 7.5-victory ace Sqn Ldr John Morgan. In February 1944 he had to bail out of a Spitfire and was captured (*R C B Ashworth*)

Spitfire VIII JF627/AN-M of No 417 Sqn was fitted with extended wingtips to enhance its high altitude performance. On 9 January 1944 Canadian ace Flg Off Garth Horricks flew an offensive patrol in this aircraft, during which he strafed locomotives. Both the aircraft and Horricks survived the war (*Canadian Forces*)

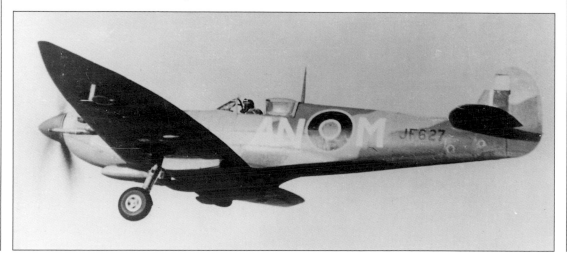

Before joining No 92 Sqn as CO, Sqn Ldr Graham Cox was supernumerary with No 72 Sqn for a short time, flying patrols over Anzio. He is seen after one such mission on 24 January 1944. With No 92 Sqn he took his score to eight and three shared destroyed (*No 72 Sqn Records*)

WO Bobby Bunting of No 93 Sqn shot down a pair of Bf 109s near Rome on 24 March 1944. The canopy from one of his victims can clearly be seen falling away in this gun camera image. Three days later, however, Bunting was wounded, and he did not return to duty until the summer (*via C F Shores*)

final victories for both aces. Another ace who made his final claims was No 601 Sqn's SAAF CO, Maj Bennie Osler, who, on the 15th, used JF722 to attack an observation balloon covered by two Bf 109s. He shot down all three. Osler was hit by flak, however, and had to put down on the beachhead strip. Running into a bomb crater, he somersaulted his aircraft. Osler escaped with minor injuries and recovered after ten days in hospital.

Forty-eight hours earlier, WO Bill Downer of No 93 Sqn had claimed his first victory over Anzio when he destroyed a Bf 109, so beginning his path to acedom as his CO, Jerry Westenra, noted;

'It was when the testing time came, over the Anzio beachhead, that Downer showed his true quality. He opened his score on 13 February by destroying an Me 109, following this on 16 February with an Fw 190. He then got another Focke-Wulf on the 19th, giving him three victories in a week.'

'Rosie' Mackie had left No 92 Sqn in mid-February, being replaced by fellow ace Sqn Ldr Graham Cox. One of Cox's flight commanders was 'Eddie' Edwards, who had succeeded desert ace Maurice Hards. On 16 February a patrol from No 92 Sqn spotted 20+ Fw 190 dive-bombers, with top cover of Bf 109s, heading for Anzio, and as they dived No 92 Sqn's Spitfires followed. Edwards and his wingman quickly caught a pair of Fw 190s. Known for his accurate gunnery, the former sent the aircraft flaming into the ground from a range of 500 yards. It was his first Spitfire victory. In the same battle Flg Off Bruce Ingalls was also successful when he too shot down an Fw 190 to claim his all-important fifth victory. Four days later he claimed another over the beachhead.

Almost at the end of his tour, No 43 Sqn's CO, Battle of Britain ace Sqn Ldr Peter Parrott, was west of Lake Albano late on the 17th when he spotted enemy aircraft;

'I was leading four Spitfires on a patrol of the Anzio beaches at about 11,000 ft. Two miles west of Lake Albano I noticed some Me 109s heading into cloud with the apparent intention of jumping us from behind. On turning about I saw an Me 109 on the tail of a Spitfire. As I saw him he broke away and dived down in front of me. I turned after him and gave him a two-second burst at about 200 yards. I saw strikes on the fuselage behind the cockpit.'

By the end of 1943 a number of Spitfire squadrons in Italy had retrained for fighter-bomber duties, among them being No 2 Sqn SAAF. This Spitfire VC gaggle armed with 250-lb bombs was photographed heading for a target at around the time (January 1944) six-victory ace Maj Harry Gaynor became CO of the unit (SAAF)

Having run out of ammunition, Parrott could only claim it damaged.

'Eddie' Edwards had further success in the Rome area before the end of the month, while the Leap Year, 29 February, proved to be expensive for the Luftwaffe, as over Cisterna WO Bobby Bunting of No 93 Sqn shot down a brace of Fw 190s to begin his rise to acedom.

There were now several changes in command at this time too, Edwards being promoted and given No 274 Sqn, although his tenure in Italy was brief;

'I had to go to the other side of Italy and return to flying older Spitfires, but I was happy. Anyway, on 17 March I was doing a strafing show up near Rome when my Spitfire got a glycol leak over the mountains. I was going to bail out but I was too low to get over the peaks. I decided to try and force-land, but as I was coming in to land the engine blew up and I don't remember anything after that.'

It was the end of Edwards' tour in Italy, however, as upon his return the unit was ordered back to the UK. No 2 Sqn SAAF also lost its CO in early March when, flying a ground attack mission near Carsoli, Maj Harry Gaynor hit high-tension cables and the ace crashed to his death. At the same time, however, the RAF's leading ace in the Mediterranean, Sqn Ldr Neville Duke, arrived as CO of No 145 Sqn, writing, 'A good squadron with an excellent record. It had a score of 196, which will doubtless increase significantly'. His youthful enthusiasm and superstitions also appeared in his diary. 'A new aircraft arrived for me this morning, a Spit VIII. Am having the letter "J" put on – hope it's lucky!' Needless to say, it was!

THE LAST BIG BATTLES

The improving weather resulted in some large scale combats as the enemy threw much of its remaining air power into blunting the Allies at Cassino and Anzio. On 7 March No 601 Sqn had a successful morning, engaging ten fighters and claiming three destroyed, one of which fell to Flg Off

Desmond Ibbotson – his tenth victory. Another became Flt Lt 'Hindoo' Henderson's fourth, but he was then shot down and killed.

Four days later No 601 Sqn paired with No 145 Sqn for an early morning patrol and intercepted a large formation over Cisterna. While the Fw 190s of SG 4 bombed, their escorts attempted to ward off the Spitfires, but two Focke-Wulfs and a Bf 109 were claimed destroyed. During the day a rare air combat opportunity arose for No 4 Sqn SAAF during an escort, when enemy aircraft were spotted taking off from Perugia. Lts 'Tank' Odendaal and D M Scott gave chase and shot down a Ju 88. The following day, while escorting Baltimores, the unit's Lt Sutton destroyed a Bf 109 before he too was shot down and killed. On the 14th Lt Sydney Richards claimed No 1 Sqn SAAF's first victory of 1944 when he destroyed an Me 410 off Penna Point.

Many SAAF pilots had distinguished careers in the Mediterranean, not least Maj John Gasson (standing on the ground second from left), who joined the crack No 92 Sqn in mid-1943 and ended the war as its CO with five victories, together with a DSO and a DFC and bar (*SAAF*)

Battles with the *Jabos* continued on almost a daily basis, such as on 24 March when, led by Neville Duke during two patrols, No 145 Sqn fought with 30+ enemy fighters over the Cassino area and claimed five destroyed, so taking the unit's wartime total beyond the 200 mark. Three days later, to the north of Rome, No 93 Sqn's Canadian Bill Downer became an ace in spectacular style when he destroyed a pair of Fw 190s. His Australian squadronmate Bobby Bunting was also involved with 50+ enemy fighters over Cassino, and his Spitfire was badly hit. Although wounded in the right leg by cannon fire, Bunting still landed safely.

On 29 March a long serving pilot finally 'broke his duck'. Plt Off Jack Doyle, who had been with No 417 Sqn for some time, was on his 185th sortie when, over Anzio, he shot down a Bf 109 to claim his first victory. His fighter was then attacked and set on fire, but despite this he managed to engage and probably destroy an Fw 190. Wounded in several places, Doyle crash-landed in the Nettuno beachhead. He eventually

Gasson's squadron flew the superb Spitfire VIII for more than two years, using the aircraft to inflict heavy losses on the Luftwaffe over Italy. Indeed, No 92 Sqn ended the war as one of the RAF's top-scoring units, although by the time MT648/QJ-Q was photographed, opportunities to add to that tally were few and very fleeting (*Peter Arnold Collection*)

achieved acedom in 1949 whilst flying with the Israelis, when, ironically, one of his victims was an Egyptian Spitfire IX!

An example of the intensity of effort to defend the troops from air attack can be shown by No 145 Sqn, which flew 32 sorties over Anzio on 3 April. On the 12th No 93 Sqn's James Andrew made his final claims in a combat near Anzio when he shot down a Bf 109 and damaged another. Sadly, during another patrol off Anzio on 16 April, ace WO Bill Downer misjudged his height, crashed into the sea and was killed.

The previous day future ace Leighton Montgomerie of No 92 Sqn, having reverted to the rank of flying officer for a second tour, had gained his second victory when, over Vitrerbo, he shot down a Bf 109. He was successful again on St George's Day (23 April) when No 92 Sqn destroyed three fighters south of Avezzano. Capt John Gasson's Fw 190 kill took him to acedom, whilst Montgomerie had the interesting experience of flying alongside the Bf 109 he had just set on fire and watching the enemy pilot bail out, 'with what was suspiciously like a wave of the hand!'

By now No 322 Wing, with Nos 154, 232 and 242 Sqns, had moved over to Alto, on Corsica, for operations alongside the USAAF's Twelfth Air Force over the northwest coast of Italy and southern France. A few days later Tarquinia was attacked, where Maj Langerman claimed one of the four Fw 190s destroyed, and on 19 April it moved on to Poretta. From there the newly arrived No 451 Sqn flew its first operational sorties over enemy territory when, on 23 April, ten Spitfire IXs escorted USAAF B-25s that were attacked as they came off the target.

The only contact made during this mission was by the sections led by the No 251 Wing Leader, Wg Cdr E J Morris, and by desert ace Flt Lt Don McBurnie. Morris attacked one of the Bf 109s three times, after which his wingman

JF476/QJ-D was amongst the first Spitfire VIIIs to reach No 92 Sqn at Canne, where it is seen on 26 November 1943. The following February Capt John Gasson was flying it near Anzio when he engaged a Bf 109 that became the second of his five victories. The aircraft did not last long, however, as it was lost a short while later following an in-flight engine failure (*P H T Green collection*)

Like most Wing Leaders, 'Teddy' Morris of No 251 Wing used his initials to identify his aircraft. He used an earlier 'TM' (Spitfire IX MK187) to claim his final two victories in June 1944, but it was then replaced by a new Spitfire IX, PL348, which he took with his wing to France. His aircraft was photographed at Cuers in September 1944 (*RAAF*)

fired twice. The enemy fighter rolled over, burst into flames and crashed, so taking 'Teddy' Morris to acedom. Later that same day eight Spitfires flew an armed reconnaissance of Leghorn, and so began an intense period of ground attack activity over Italy and the Mediterranean. These sorties mainly took the form of armed reconnaissance and bomber escort missions (including some for French B-26s) and these continued into May.

Allied fighters were increasingly the masters of Italian skies, with one of the most successful combats being carried out by No 72 Sqn on 7 May. Led by CO Sqn Ldr 'Duke' Arthur, the unit engaged a large formation of Bf 109s from I./JG 4 south of Lake Bracciano. Enemy aircraft quickly began to fall, one of which was claimed by Flt Lt Basil

Pilots from No 72 Sqn pose for the camera following their outstanding combat on 7 May, when they shot down nine Bf 109s in four minutes. Sitting on the Spitfire's nose, from left to right, are Flt Sgt J T Aspinal (one kill), Flg Off Bruce Hendry (two) and Sgt Jeff Bird (two), sitting on the wing are Lt Petrus van Schalkwyk (two) and Flt Lt Basil Blackburn (two), and standing is the CO, Sqn Ldr 'Duke' Arthur (one). This victory was the fourth of Arthur's six successes (*No 72 Sqn Records*)

During the highly successful 7 May combat Petrus van Schalkwyk flew Spitfire IX MK171/RN-O. He was also at its controls for the fighter's first sortie with the squadron on 15 April. Finally, he was almost certainly sitting in the aircraft's cockpit when this photograph was taken at Lago on 19 April. Van Schalkwyk ended his tour with four victories, and he served in the SAAF post-war. MK171 was wrecked in an accident in January 1945 (*P H T Green Collection*)

Blackburn. He noted in his log book 'Our big day! We bounced 18 '109s and got nine of them. I got one'. It was his fourth victory, but frustratingly the fifth never came. Arthur claimed his fourth, Flg Off Aspinal got another, while his fellow New Zealander Flg Off R B Hendry shot down two, as did Lt Petrus van Schalkwyk and Sgt 'Dickie' Bird. The latter recalled the first of his three victories;

'I followed a '109 to low level before hitting him. He actually exploded and I flew through the fire and smoke, which was recorded on the camera. The wreckage crashed some miles north of the lake.'

Then on 11 May, on a 20-mile front, the British 8th and US 5th Armies opened the Fourth Battle of Cassino in what was hoped to be the final assault on the *Gustav* Line and the advance on Rome. With the line breached, the forces at Anzio would break out and cut off the retreating German 10th Army in the Alban Hills before they could establish a line before Rome. The days following the offensive would see the Spitfire squadrons engage and utterly defeat the enemy *Jabos*.

On the 13th Neville Duke claimed his first victory over Italy during a sweep deep into enemy territory;

'Great things at last! We met up with six Me 109s over Arezzo, the other side of Perugia (near Florence). There were six of us and we had a good dice. I got a burst at one and saw strikes under its belly before he rolled down and off. Stayed up and dodged and turned for a bit, finally fixing onto one up above, whom I climbed and turned with, easily climbing and out-turning him. I could see him flicking on the stall – he throttled back and straightened out, kicking his tail and skidding violently. Observed strikes in fuselage and forward around the engine cowl. Pieces started coming off as enemy aircraft went down in a wide spiral. Lost sight but saw explosion where it had disappeared.'

A contemporary press account described the fight from the perspective of another No 145 Sqn pilot;

'At dusk today 22-year-old Flt Sgt Colin (Jock) Stirling climbed out of his Spitfire on an advanced airfield in Italy and reported that, single handed, he had taken on four Me 109s over the battle area, destroying one, probably destroying a second and damaging a third.'

In May 1944 No 253 Sqn at Foggia flew mainly ground attack missions under the command of Sqn Ldr Paul Webb, who had become an ace flying Spitfires with No 602 Sqn during the Battle of Britain (*No 253 Sqn Records*)

Spitfire IX MJ282/JU-A of No 111 Sqn prepares to start up prior to another patrol in the spring of 1944. On 14 May Flt Lt R L Brook destroyed a Bf 109 while flying this aircraft, and nine days later Flg Off Bray damaged a Bf 109. The aircraft later served with No 601 Sqn and No 3 Sqn SAAF, and it also survived the war (*T Hooton*)

Over the next few days the fighter-bombers of SG 4 and SKG 10 suffered further losses from various units, including the penultimate victory for No 92 Sqn's CO, Sqn Ldr Graham Cox. By the 18th the *Gustav* line had cracked and the 8th Army streamed across the River Rapido into the Liri valley. The race to clear the *Hitler* Line beyond and then Rome was on! In the skies above and behind the frontline the battle remained deadly for the enemy, and it was certainly No 145 Sqn's day on 21 May when, in the evening, it ran into 20 Fw 190s. Duke shot down two while Flg Off Joe Ekbery chased three more. The unit diary described how the 23-year-old Lancastrian became an ace;

'Flg Off J S Ekbery chased three Fw 190s. He fired on one in a dive at 3000 ft from 200 yards, hitting it in the port wing and fuselage, and black smoke poured from the enemy aircraft as it went down from 1000 ft like a falling leaf. He then turned into a second Fw 190 and lost sight of the first. Firing at the second enemy aircraft from 200 yards astern, he saw strikes on its fuselage and wings and the pilot bailed out at 1000 ft. He then saw a third Fw 190 turning to port six miles east of Rome at 500 ft. Catching him up rapidly, he fired from 150 yards quarter astern, striking the fuselage and port wing. The enemy aircraft went into a vertical dive and crashed.'

The squadron claimed eight Fw 190s destroyed during the day – an unsustainable loss rate for the enemy.

By 25 May Allied forces coming up from the south were finally able to join up with the developing breakout from Anzio-Nettuno, and there was intense air combat over central Italy. Flying from Corsica, No 242 Sqn attacked eight Fw 190s over Viterbo aerodrome. Claiming one of the four destroyed was Flt Sgt Eric Doherty, making him an ace.

Having achieved his first claim as far back as August 1940, No 243 Sqn's Flt Lt Cyril Bamberger also finally achieved his fifth victory that same day when, over Viterbo, he shot down a Bf 109 that blew up after his attack. On 27 May, whilst flying with No 1 Sqn SAAF, Lt Col Andrew Bosman claimed his final victories when he destroyed a pair of Bf 109s near Foligno – they were probably from 1° *Gruppo CT* of the Fascist Repubblica Sociale Italiana (RSI). By the end of May the Luftwaffe and the RSI's *Aeronautica Nazionale Repubblicana* (ANR) had been routed in central Italy, having taken a fearful beating and sustaining crippling losses. On the 29th SG 4 began withdrawing.

Rome fell on 4 June, and with the Luftwaffe now largely absent from Italian skies, many fighter squadrons switched to ground attack work, with a resulting rise in casualties. Such was the random nature that on the 7th Neville Duke, having hit a purple patch by achieving five victories in May, was shot down by flak and bailed out into Lake Bracciano. Unable to release his parachute harness, he almost drowned.

Enemy aircraft continued to be encountered, although not in large numbers, especially following the Allied landings in Normandy. Nevertheless, on 8 June Wg Cdr 'Teddy' Morris led No 451 Sqn in an armed reconnaissance, and near Poggibonsi he spotted a Ju 88. The unit chased it for 60 miles to the south of Siena before Morris and Flt Lt Sutton set the starboard engine on fire. Ju 88T-1 Wk-Nr 430913 '4U+HG' of 1.(F)/123 pulled up to port, parts of its canopy flew off and it crashed in flames with Oberfahnrich Scherpf and crew.

Leader of No 251 Wing for much of 1944, Wg Cdr 'Teddy' Morris was a South African pilot in the RAF. Most of his seven victories were shared, including his fifth success on 23 April – a Bf 109 that he and his wingman destroyed over Lake Trasimento. Morris had been leading No 451 Sqn from Corsica at the time, the unit escorting USAAF B-25s in a raid on Italy (*Ian Simpson*)

On the 14th Morris led six Spitfires from No 451 Sqn as cover to 36 B-25s of the 310th BG that were attacking a viaduct near Pistoia. Jumped by Bf 109s, he went after the leader and hit him around the cockpit and engine – pieces flew off and the fighter turned onto its back and went in, giving Morris his seventh victory. The following day the No 322 Wing Leader, and one of the RAF's most able but least known aces, Wg Cdr Tony Lovell led No 243 Sqn in a fight with a formation of ANR fighters south of Piacenza. He shot down the Fiat G.55 of 1° *Gruppo's* Sottotenente Morettin, who bailed out but died of his wounds. It was Lovell's 22nd, and last, victory.

There were occasional encounters such as on 19 July, when Flt Lt Paddy Turkington, now with No 241 Sqn (a tactical reconnaissance unit), was flying near Ancona. Sighting two Bf 109s, he gave chase and eventually opened fire, causing his target to burst into flames and the pilot to bail out – he shot down three more Bf 109s before the end of the month. The following day Sqn Ldr Graham Cox claimed his 11th victory when he downed Ju 188D-2 Wk-Nr 290183 'F6+HM' of 4.(F)/122, flown by Oberleutnant Fritz Muller. The Spitfires had spotted the Junkers some 7000 ft above them, and climbing to 27,000 ft Cox attacked from below, setting the engines on fire, and it crashed near Cervarezza.

OPERATION DRAGOON

'The Luftwaffe can be virtually ignored'. Thus pronounced Air Marshal John Slessor, C-in-C RAF Mediterranean and Middle East, on 10 July 1944 when assessing the prospects for Operation *Dragoon* – the Allied landings on the French Riviera that it was hoped would draw German forces away from the fighting in Normandy. The initial air cover was provided by carrier-borne fighters, but in addition to No 332 (French) Wing, other Spitfire wings were moved to Corsica to fly preparatory operations. Italian-based units like No 145 Sqn also directly supported *Dragoon*.

Having recovered from his wounds, WO Bobby Bunting had rejoined No 93 Sqn in Corsica. During a last light patrol over the French Riviera on 27 July he became an ace when, over the sea to the south of Nice, he intercepted an Me 410 and its two Fw 190 escorts. Bunting managed to shoot one of the latter down.

During the first fortnight of August intensive patrols were flown over southern France in preparation for the landings, which took place on the 15th. No 72's Sqn Ldr 'Duke' Arthur witnessed the landings;

'As we wheeled away the clouds broke enough for us to see hundreds of ships steaming in to pour troops ashore. We saw smoke and flame belching from the warships as heavy cannon roared into action, pounding what gun defences were left. No enemy fighters showed.'

Other notable pilots also flew over this new front as well. For example, on the 22nd a sweep by No 111 Sqn included several 'guests' (almost all of them aces), including Gp Capt Wilf Duncan-Smith, Wg Cdr Barry Heath and Sqn Ldrs 'Hunk' Humphries, 'Chips' Carpenter, Graham Cox and Neville Duke – a pretty impressive bunch! Patrols over the French coastal areas continued for a time, and towards the end of August No 324 Wing (Nos 43, 72, 93 and 111 Sqns) and the French wing moved into France. Soon afterwards most of the other Corsican-based squadrons were disbanded.

THE LAST RITES

The Allied breakout from Normandy and massive pressure on the Eastern Front left little enemy air power for the Italian front as the Allies slowly moved northwards from Rome. Florence was taken in early August, but to the north across the rugged mountains of northern Italy, the enemy had established the *Gothic* Line, which was clearly going to be difficult to break. However, the 8th Army was to thrust in the east towards the Po Valley, supported by the DAF squadrons, but the skies above were no sinecure for the ground attack units and the loss rate spiralled.

Shortage of aviation fuel now began to have a serious effect on operations, with the ANR flying its last missions for more than two months on 10 August as the Luftwaffe commandeered its fuel. No 92 Sqn celebrated another ace in its ranks on 25 August when, during a dawn patrol over La Spezia naval base, Flt Lt Leighton Montgomerie downed a reconnaissance Bf 109 of 2./NAGr 11. He was the last pilot to 'make ace' flying a Spitfire in the Mediterranean theatre. Tragically, it was but a brief glory, for the next day he scrambled after a reconnaissance Me 410 but when landing his engine failed and he crashed. Critically injured, he died the next day. Neville Duke wrote an epitaph in his diary;

'Bad news this morning that "Monty" in 92 has been killed trying to force land short of fuel on the 'drome over at Rosignano. Shame. Montgomery was one of the better types in life.'

During early September the last Luftwaffe fighter units departed Italy, leaving the country's aerial defence in the hands of the newly reformed ANR. German night attack and reconnaissance units remained, however, and it was Bf 109 nightfighters that Neville Duke encountered on 3 September near Ravenna;

Following the successful Allied landings in southern France, No 43 Sqn was one of the first Spitfire units to be based in the country. It initially moved to Ramatuelle, on the Cote d'Azur, where the Merlin engine of Spitfire IX MT714/FT-F is being serviced on 23 August (*P H T Green Collection*)

'Closed in, after a long chase. Took the left hand chap and fired at long range and got a strike in the first burst behind the cockpit. Closed, firing another burst, and hood and pilot bailed out. Chased after other two '109s, easily closing in with leader. Fired, and after a couple of bursts got hits in fuselage and he caught fire. Later the pilot bailed out.'

Duke's final kills made him the top scoring Allied fighter pilot in the Mediterranean theatre, the 22-year-old being credited with a total of 27 and two shared victories, one probable and six damaged during the course of 486 sorties in 712 hours on operations. They were also No 145 Sqn's final victories. Duke left for the UK shortly afterwards, being replaced by another ace, Sqn Ldr 'Dan' Daniel.

A rare opportunity for No 1 Sqn SAAF came on 10 September when, near Bologna, a section led by Capt Don Brebner caught an Me 410. He opened fire and it slowed. Another burst set the starboard engine on fire, and Brebner's wingmen finished the aircraft off. This share took Don Brebner's total to four. It was also the squadron's final victory, taking its total to 165.5. A little over a month later, on 14 October, No 72 Sqn's CO, Sqn Ldr 'Duke' Arthur, and five other pilots destroyed a Ju 188D-2 of 6.(F)/122 (though identified as an Me 410). His share is thought to be the final victory scored by an ace in a Spitfire in the Mediterranean. Flak and the weather were by now the main threat, and as if to reinforce this point No 601 Sqn ace Flt Lt Desmond Ibbotson was killed in a flying accident in mid-November.

The reconstituted ANR did contest some raids, occasionally quite effectively, but the Allies were now the undoubted masters of Italian skies. Spitfire pilots occasionally encountered Italian machines, with the first contact of 1945 coming on 23 January when the No 244 Wing Leader, desert ace Wg Cdr Ron Bary, was leading 417 Sqn. No claims were made after the brief skirmish, although in fact Tenente Filippi of 2ª *Squadriglia* was mortally wounded

When SAAF Marauders attacking the Conegliano marshalling yards on 3 March, they were intercepted by ANR Bf 109s near Pordenone. These were in turn engaged by the escorting Spitfires from No 4 Sqn SAAF. Lt M F Reim, who was 'tail end charlie', was credited with an 'Fw 190' shot down before he was hit over Oderzo and had to bail out. The Spitfire's final claim over Italy had a tragic twist, for Reim was murdered when trying to evade capture.

Flt Lt Desmond Ibbotson achieved all bar two of his eleven victories flying Spitfires with No 601 Sqn over the desert and Italy, his last coming in the heavy fighting over Anzio in the spring of 1944. Sadly, on 19 November, towards the end of his second tour, he was killed in a flying accident (*C Rowley*)

For much of the last year of the war the veteran No 601 Sqn flew on fighter-bomber duties. Here, Spitfire IXs MJ532/UF-G and MJ250/UF-Q, each fitted with 250-lb bombs, accelerate down the runway at Fano. Both fighters still wear the squadron badge, but MJ250 is unusual for not being camouflaged. This machine was regularly flown by Desmond Ibbotson prior to his death (*C Rowley*)

OVER THE AEGEAN
AND THE BALKANS

During its invasion of Greece in 1940, Italy also seized the Dodecanese islands in the Aegean, and following the Italian surrender in early September 1943 the Allies attempted to occupy them. However, before British troops could be landed on the largest island of Rhodes, on 11 September the Germans seized control. Nevertheless, the governors of nearby Kos, Leros and Samos agreed to accept British garrisons. The units earmarked for the islands included two fighter squadrons that were to be based on Kos, although German occupation of Rhodes effectively gave them a degree of air superiority.

On the 13th the leading elements of No 7 Sqn SAAF, with six Spitfire Vs, moved across to Antimachina, with further aircraft arriving the next day. The squadron was commanded by a great SAAF character, Maj Corrie van Vliet, who had several victories to his name from his earlier service in the desert. Leros was occupied on the 15th when, from first light, a standing patrol of two Spitfires was maintained over Kos to cover the transport aircraft and ships delivering stores and reinforcements. However, the Germans reacted quickly, and Kos and Leros were ordered to be taken. The air bombardment began on 17 September, with the defending South African pilots giving a good account of themselves. One was Lt Ray Burl, who in a newspaper interview in May 1977 recalled attacking a Ju 52/3m that day;

'To the aircrews in a formation of Junkers 52s, droning their way above the shimmering Aegean on a brilliant afternoon, the realities of war must have seemed far away indeed. That was probably their assumption – and this may have accounted for the fact that their escort of Ju 88s was far ahead and hopelessly out of position to offer them protection. The tranquility of the afternoon was shattered as our two Spitfire Vs dived out of the sun and guns blazing fell upon the formation of ponderous transports. Flames and smoke soon erupted from one of the JU 52s, and the stricken aircraft flipped abruptly and plunged to its destruction in the sea.'

However, Burl was hit by return fire and had to land. Two days later No 7 Sqn SAAF's Spitfires engaged Bf 109s of 10./JG 27, downing two, but at a cost of Lts Turner and Cheesman. On the 19th Lt Seel, having downed a Bf 109, spun into the sea while chasing another and was killed.

The action in the air intensified over succeeding days, with attacks on Leros beginning on the 26th. The next day Corrie van Vliet destroyed a Bf 109G – believed to have been the aircraft of Unteroffizier Jakob Hervez of III./JG 27. A Ju 88 also fell, taking No 7 Sqn SAAF's tally over Kos to at least a dozen. By now a detachment from No 74 Sqn, led by its ace CO, Sqn Ldr Jim Hayter, had arrived, and on the 29th Flt Sgt Wilson shot down a Ju 88, then apparently caused two Bf 109s to collide!

No 94 Sqn's CO Sqn Ldr Russ
Foskett closes up alongside a
Beaufighter of No 603 Sqn in his
Spitfire VC MH558/GO-C while
escorting the unit during its attack
on the radar station at Rhodes on
5 May 1944. He claimed his seventh,
and last, victory a month later,
although his squadron continued
flying escort missions over the
Aegean area well into late 1944
(*Ian Simpson*)

However, it was too little, too late as on 3 October the Germans conducted amphibious and airborne landings, taking the main town later that day. The British withdrew from Kos under the cover of darkness and surrendered the next day, survivors having to make their escape by whatever means could be found. This was followed by landings on Leros on 12 November, and British forces on the island capitulated four days later. It was one of the last German successes of the war.

The following year a flight was formed for the operational testing of the Spitfire floatplane for potential use from island bases in the Aegean. Three Spitfire VB floatplanes were delivered to No 71 OTU, which established a Floatplane Flight at Fanora, on the Great Bitter Lake. The flight comprised five experienced Spitfire pilots and 15 groundcrew under the command of Flt Lt Willie Lindsay (a six-victory ace from the Tunisian campaign). Only two Spitfires – EP751 and EP754 – were assembled, Lindsay making the first flight when he eased EP751 off the waters of the lake for a familiarisation sortie on 2 December 1944.

The fighters were flown regularly until the planned operational deployment was cancelled in mid-December. Lindsay flew his last sortie on the 13th when he and another pilot practised formation flying and water landings. The aircraft were then crated up and returned to Britain and the pilots posted to other duties – another tour of operations with No 242 Sqn in the case of Willie Lindsay.

The defeat at Kos was not the last time that Spitfires were seen in the skies over the Aegean, for they occasionally escorted bombers sent to attack targets in the Dodecanese islands. Flying from bases in Cyprus and Egypt, among the units involved was No 94 Sqn, under Sqn Ldr Russ Foskett. It had commenced swapping its Spitfire VBs for IXs in early 1944, and in April the unit moved into Bu Amud. No 94 Sqn began operations on the 16th when it escorted Marauders of No 24 Sqn SAAF that had been tasked with attacking shipping in the port of Heraklion, on Crete. This type of activity was the norm. For example, on 7 May seven Spitfires, led by Foskett, escorted No 603 Sqn's Beaufighters on an attack against a radar station on Rhodes. A month later, on 6 June, Russ Foskett intercepted a Ju 52/3m over the Mediterranean and forced it down at Tmimi, in Libya, where it was captured. His first success in a Spitfire took his total to 6.5 victories.

During his last months as CO of No 249 Sqn, Sqn Ldr E N Woods flew Spitfire VC JK465/GN-X. He made his first flight in it (a cannon test) from Italian soil on 28 October 1943 (*D A S Colvin*)

E N 'Timber' Woods, now a wing commander and the leader of No 286 Wing, ruefully examines the damage inflicted to the propeller of his Spitfire on 4 December 1943. His fighter was hit by flak shortly before he downed a Ju 87 over Podgorica for his final victory. Sadly, Woods went missing over Yugoslavia in bad weather on 16 December, having possibly collided with his wingman (*D A S Colvin*)

During No 94 Sqn's escort operations, it claimed four Bf 109s destroyed, the last falling on 10 August 1944 to Lt Cdr Stanic (the first Yugoslav pilot serving in the RAF to score an aerial victory). In the same action over Crete Sqn Ldr Foskett damaged a Bf 109.

– OVER THE BALKANS –

Since invading Yugoslavia in 1941 the Germans had been fighting a partisan army. The Allies were keen to support their activities, so once it was established in Italy in the autumn of 1943 the RAF formed the Balkan Air Force (BAF) to control activities across the Adriatic. The Luftwaffe largely fielded attack aircraft in this theatre, so there was little opportunity for air combat. Indeed, the main task for Spitfire and, later, Mustang squadrons was ground attack and interdiction.

One of the Spitfire units that concentrated on Balkan operations was No 249 Sqn, led by 11-victory ace Sqn Ldr E N 'Timber' Woods. He flew its first operation after moving to Italy on 2 November, leading a sweep north of Durazzo. A few days later, whilst on a B-25 escort, Woods noted in his log book, 'Wizard bombing – shot up two schooners on return'. After a sortie later in the month he also noted with some prescience, 'Eight lorries on fire – plenty of flak – five aircraft hit'.

No 249 Sqn claimed its first victory over Yugoslavia on 17 November when Flt Sgt Dale downed a Bf 109 near Berat. The next afternoon, when leading No 232 Sqn over Tivat Bay, on the Albanian coast, Gp Capt 'Dutch' Hugo achieved his 19th, and last, kill when he spotted a lone Ar 196 floatplane;

'I caught up with the aircraft, flying at a height of 100 ft, about eight miles due south of Tivat and about 200 yards offshore. At 250 yards I opened fire with cannon and machine guns, almost immediately scoring hits on the port float, which caught fire, and the port wing and fuselage. The aircraft turned slightly left, and the engine and whole fuselage caught fire. Just as I stopped firing and broke away, the aircraft blew up. After straightening up from the break-away, I saw most of the aircraft on fire crash into the sea very close inshore, with other fragments falling around it and a few fragments on shore.'

Unteroffizier Paul Rogge and Leutnant Frederick Kellner of SAGr 126 were both killed.

No 249 Sqn had several successes in early December, one

coming on the afternoon of the 2nd, as Flt Lt Derek Colvin described to the author;

'I was leading a section of Spits on a sweep up the Dalmatian coast in fairly poor weather when, north of the Albanian port of Valona, we spotted an Me 109 – quite an unusual occurrence by then. Anyhow, I managed to get close enough to loose off a couple of bursts and saw smoke pouring from it before pulling off. One of the other chaps then had a squirt and the enemy pilot bailed out and the ME dived into the ground and exploded in flames.'

By now Woods had been promoted to lead No 286 Wing, and two days later he was over Yugoslavia, as he described in his report;

'I was making a recce of Podgorica aerodrome. I was on the north side of the aerodrome at zero feet when I saw a Ju 87 coming towards me at 500 ft. Just at this moment all the ground defences opened fire and I was hit almost immediately by Bofors in the airscrew, causing the whole aircraft to vibrate intensely. I climbed underneath the Ju 87, which dived to ground level and took violent evasive action, while the rear gunner opened fire completely out of range. I chased the enemy aircraft for about three miles, and opened fire at about 250 yards with about a half ring of deflection. I gave a four-second burst and a large lump came off the starboard wing. I also saw strikes on the cockpit. Return fire ceased and the enemy aircraft dived into the ground and blew up.'

Sadly, on 16 December, both Woods and Sqn Ldr K B L Debenham, OC No 126 Sqn, were killed during a sweep over Yugoslavia. It appears that they may have collided with one another in poor weather.

Another ex-Malta Spitfire unit now in Italy was No 1435 Sqn, which during November 1943 re-equipped with Spitfire IXs. On the 17th, when covering a rescue operation off Albania for a No 249 Sqn pilot,

On 17 November 1943 No 1435 Sqn fought a very successful action off the Albanian coast that resulted in four Bf 109s being shot down. Two fell to New Zealander Flt Lt Warren Schrader, who is seen here sitting on the gun barrel of his Spitfire. On the left is his CO, Sqn Ldr Richard Webb, who also claimed a Bf 109, and on the right is Flt Sgt Butler, who bagged the fourth (via C H Thomas)

Spitfire IX MH660/Y-V of No 1435 Sqn acts as a handsome backdrop for a photograph! In addition to a squadron badge on the fin, its pilot has decorated the aircraft with a dragon's head under the cockpit. MH660 joined the squadron in early 1944, and it was flown on a number of occasions by future ace Flt Lt Warren Schrader (B Riglesford)

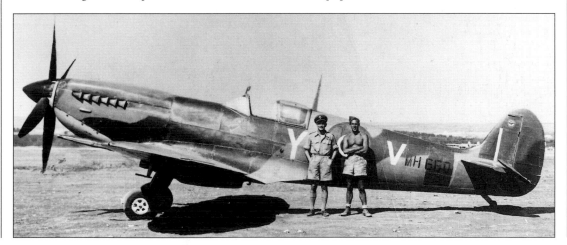

Australian ace Sqn Ldr Russ Foskett, CO of No 94 Sqn, strikes an iconic pose on the wing of his Spitfire in the summer of 1943. Sadly, on 31 October 1944, shortly after moving to Greece to support operations in the area, Foskett was lost when his Spitfire suffered an engine failure over the sea (*Ian Simpson*)

these aircraft were used to great effect, bringing down four Bf 109s. The CO, Sqn Ldr Richard Webb, claimed his third kill, while Flt Sgt Butler got another. The laurels, however, went to Flt Lt Warren Schrader, who recently described how he began his path to acedom;

'Two Me 109s came in below us and I was able to shoot them both down. The first one just blew up with my first attack, but I had to pursue the other for some time. He was taking evasive action and, for some reason, eventually bailed out. I don't know if the pilot was wounded, but his parachute opened prematurely, hit the tailplane and just streamed above him, not decelerating him much as he fell straight down and hit the ground – this was, no doubt, fatal.'

He also opened the squadron's 'book' for 1944, recalling;

'My second encounter with Me 109s happened on 3 January 1944. In this combat I learned a valuable lesson. We went into attack and I hadn't given Hoare any instructions as my No 2. I shot down the lead '109 and looked around to find Hoare still behind me, with the other '109 escaping. As I followed the first '109 down, I saw him streaming glycol and level out just above the sea. The canopy opened, and it was obvious that he was about to ditch when Hoare went in and gave him a squirt and claimed half my kill!'

Such encounters were a rarity, however, and No 249 Sqn's first victory of the year did not occur until late April when Flt Lt 'Shorty' Beatson shot down an Fi 156. The following month No 253 Sqn at Foggia welcomed an ace as its new CO when Sqn Ldr Paul Webb arrived. The unit transferred to the BAF in July, supporting Tito's partisans from the offshore island airfield at Vis.

At dawn on 25 June the Germans had launched an offensive on Tito's HQ near Drvar with considerable air support. In response, No 249 Sqn sent a section of six Spitfires and they shot down four Hs 126s. One was shared by Derek Colvin, who was now the CO. He saw a crewman bail out before a wing broke away and the aircraft crashed. This was No 249 Sqn's last major action on Spitfires, and soon afterward Colvin left after a very successful tour.

The Germans then began a determined offensive in Montenegro, which prompted increased attacks on enemy lines of communication, the pressure on the partisans continuing into August with fighter support.

RE-OCCUPATION OF GREECE

In September 1944 British forces returned to Greece and many airfields were secured, including Kalamaki, which became the home for No 337 Wing (and Nos 32, 73 and 94 Sqns, all with Spitfire Vs) over the next month. It began operations against the Germans as they retreated northwards, but sadly soon after arriving No 94 Sqn's CO Russ Foskett was lost when his Spitfire developed engine problems after strafing trains near Prokhama and he had to bail out over the sea. He was not found.

To increase the range of its aircraft No 94 Sqn began using Sedes, 150 miles to the north, for refuelling and rearming, and from here it had occasional brushes with unusual opponents such as the Bulgarian Bf 109 over the Vardar valley that Flt Lt Graham Hulse hit on 12 November. At the end of the month Sqn Ldr Jack Slade took over No 94 Sqn, but air combat opportunities remained both fleeting and few.

VICTORY!

By March 1945 the enemy had effectively been swept from the skies above Italy and the Balkans. This in turn meant that Spitfire units primarily flew ground attack missions in order to keep themselves busy. As the war in Italy entered its final phase, the Germans were entrenched on the banks of the River Senio, and British troops needed strong air support to help the drive across the River Po. No 601 Sqn's tasks were typical of those assigned to the Spitfire units, with attacks being made against enemy lines of communications, particularly bridges and ferries across the Po.

Sadly, losses on these missions continued. On 12 April the No 244 Wing Leader, Wg Cdr Ron Bary, flew on a ground attack operation with No 92 Sqn against a target near Imola. However, as he tipped into the dive his aircraft exploded and crashed – one of his bombs had almost certainly detonated prematurely. A tragic end to a long operational career, Bary was the last ace to die in a Spitfire in the Mediterranean.

There were, however, still occasional encounters with enemy aircraft over Yugoslavia as the Germans attempted to extricate themselves from the Balkans. No 73 Sqn, under the command of SAAF ace Maj Doug Golding, had some success, and during an early morning patrol over Croatia on 9 March SAAF pilot Capt W J Marits damaged a twin-engined aircraft south of Zagreb. In the same area that day Flg Off Reggie Letts also shot down an ancient Caproni Ca.133. Yugoslav-manned No 352 Sqn shot down a Hs 126 on the 20th, this being claimed by Sqn Ldr Hinko Sojic. Ten days later, to the north of Gospic, No 73 Sqn got in on the action once more when an early morning patrol encountered a trio of veteran Do 17s, and their fighter escorts. They were promptly attacked, Flg Off Norm Pearce destroying one of them and Lt Harper damaged one of the escorts.

By this time a civil war had erupted in nearby Greece, and one of the RAF units based in the country at the time was No 94 Sqn. Among its pilots was Rhodesian Flg Off Rodney Simmonds, who described one of the Spitfire's last victories in the Mediterranean to the author;

'The incident occurred on 31 March 1945 when I was with No 94 Sqn in Greece. I was flying with the CO (Sqn Ldr John Slade) and two others whose names I cannot remember. The four of us were returning from the Turkish border along the Bulgarian border when we came across a Me 109 stooging along ahead of us at the same height. We couldn't believe our luck, and the CO, without

By early 1945, after a long operational career, Wg Cdr Ron Bary was the Leader of No 244 Wing. Tragically, shortly before the German surrender in Italy, a bomb he dropped detonated prematurely, killing him instantly. He was the last ace to be lost in a Spitfire in the Mediterranean during World War 2 (*author's collection*)

On 31 March 1945, Flg Off Rodney Simmonds of No 94 Sqn was flying Spitfire IX MJ730/GO-Y when he had an 'encounter' with a Bulgarian Bf 109. The latter was shot down, but officially this event never happened! (*Rodney Simmonds*)

Every inch the archetypal fighter pilot! Wearing his Rhodesian wings, Flg Off Rodney Simmonds shared in the destruction of a lone Bulgarian Bf 109, which was, *de facto*, **one of the last Spitfire victories of the war in the Mediterranean** (*Rodney Simmonds*)

hesitation, led the attack. We all had a squirt and despatched it in flames to mother earth. As it plunged down I noticed instead of the usual German cross on the side of the fuselage it had something like an "X". At the debrief it was concluded that it was a Bulgarian air force machine.

'Regrettably, our intelligence was not fully up to date, for we had not been told that Bulgaria had capitulated to our allies, the Russians, two weeks previously, and was therefore no longer considered to be an enemy. Our indiscretions were rightly hushed up, as the problem was not an equipment malfunction but just "finger trouble" on our part!

'The attacking of a Bulgarian '109 was totally hushed up, as it was a major boob on our part. Under grave penalty we were told to shut up, and no record appeared anywhere. The incident was near Ekinos. It was even decided not to include the incident in any ORB report, and we were ordered to make no mention of it in our logbook entries. After 60 years I don't suppose it matters if I mention it now. The vagaries of war!'

Two days after this combat that officially had never happened, No 73 Sqn had further luck when, at 1830 hrs in the Karlovac area, Pearce and Harper spotted a pair of Bf 109Gs flying at 4000 ft. Promptly attacking, Harper damaged one of them and Norm Pearce (in MJ349) downed the other, as he subsequently described;

'Approximately nine miles southeast of Karlovac my leader reported two aircraft approaching from "11 o'clock" on a course approximately reciprocal to our own, and flying at "angels 4". As we drew abreast I recognised them as Me 109s. With the section, I dived to the attack.

'Closing on the aircraft, I recognised one of them as a Spitfire being fired at from astern by a Me 109 from a range of about 400 yards. The Spitfire immediately broke to port, still being fired at by the Me 109. I fired two short bursts to draw his attention from the Spitfire under attack. The enemy pilot then appeared to attempt to turn to try to attack me, but I was well positioned and gave him a two-second burst from 75 yards, raking the fuselage and cockpit. I believe the enemy pilot must have been hit as the Me 109 rolled onto its back and crashed into the ground, bursting into flames. The enemy aircraft had yellow and black mottled camouflage and bore the usual German markings.'

Following VE Day, several Spitfire units became part of the Occupation Forces, including No 253 Sqn at Treviso under the command of ace Sqn Ldr Peter Ottewill. Adorned with the squadron badge on their tails, Spitfire IXs MJ778/SW-T and MA485/SW-G are prepared for a patrol along the Italian border with Austria (*J W Gardner*)

Pearce's CO, Sqn Ldr J H Ashton, commented;

'A first class attack with excellent shooting, which undoubtedly saved the No 1 the embarrassment of being shot down. This pilot is showing great promise for the future.'

In spite of these comments, Norm Pearce recalled;

'I can recall getting a telling off from the CO for not putting more detail in my logbook. I had encountered enemy aircraft only twice during my whole time with No 73 Sqn. We spent most of our time shooting up troop convoys when one was located. I often saw my cannon shells striking the trucks, but there was never a fire in my experience. They were probably all diesel. As a result of this, I never put claims in my log.'

His modesty notwithstanding, the young Canadian had claimed No 73 Sqn's 321st, and final, 'kill' of the war. More significantly, however, this was also the Spitfire's last victory in the Mediterranean theatre.

The fighting continued in Italy, and on the 21st Bologna fell. Soon afterwards the 5th and 8th Armies linked up, trapping the 100,000 men of the German 10th Army south of the Po. The Wehrmacht in Italy signed an instrument of surrender on the 29th that became effective on 2 May 1945.

The Commander of Fighter Forces in northern Italy, the hugely able and influential fighter leader Oberst Eduard Neumann (who had also been *Kommodore* of JG 27 in North Africa in 1942-43) commented post-war on the arrival of the Spitfire in the desert;

'More impressive than the arrival of the Americans, however, was the arrival of the first Spitfires in the skies over North Africa. In my opinion it was only thanks to the merits of Marseille that we were able to reduce the unquestionable threat from this aircraft to a bearable degree.'

During the air war in the Mediterranean a total of 61 pilots had become Spitfire aces over North Africa and Italy, whilst a further 76 aces claimed at least part of their total when flying Spitfires in the area. Appropriately, therefore, the last word should go to the most successful of them all, Sqn Ldr Neville Duke;

'It is said that the Spitfire is too beautiful to be a fighting machine. I sometimes think it's true, but then what better fighter could you want?'

APPENDICES

Spitfire Aces of North Africa and Italy

Name	Service	Unit/s	Theatre Claims	Total Claims
Duke N F	RAF	92, 145	20/-/2	27+2sh/1/6
Mackie E D	RNZAF	243, 92	16+1sh/1/10+1sh	20+3sh/2/10+1sh
Daniel S W F	RAF	72, 601, 145	16+1sh/1/10	16+1sh/2/12
Hill G U	RCAF	111	10+6+1sh/2/9	10+8sh/3/10
Taylor J S	RAF	145, 601	13+2sh/2/10+2sh	13+2sh/2/10+2sh
Hussey R J H	RAF	72	9+5sh/1/4+1sh	9+5sh/1/4+1sh
Maguire W I H	Rhod	81, 154	12/1/2	13/1/2
Turkington R W	RAF	43, 324 Wg, 41, 601	9+3sh/1/4	9+3sh/1/4
Hugo P H	RAF	322 Wg	10+1sh/2/2	17+2sh/3/7
Ingram M R B	RNZAF	601, 243, 152	7+4sh/3/4	8+6sh/3/5
Gilroy G K	RAF	324 Wg	7+4sh/2sh/2+3sh +3sh dest on gnd	14+11sh/2sh/7+3sh +3sh dest on gnd
Gray C F	RAF	81, 322 Wg	10/2+2sh/1	27+2sh/7+4sh/12
Ibbotson D	RAF	601, 103 MU	9/2/3	11/4/4
Wade L S	RAF	145	10/1/9	23+2sh/1/13
Aikman A F	RCAF	154	8+2sh/1/3	8+2sh/1/4
Keith G N	RCAF	72	8+1sh/2/1	8+1sh/2/3
Berry R	RAF	81, 322 Wg	5+4sh/2/8	14+10sh/9/17
Wedgewood J H	RAF	92	8/2/9	10/2/12
Houle A U	RCAF	145, 417	8/-/3	11+1sh/1/7
Horbaczewski E	Pol	45 PFT, 43, 601	8/-/1	6+1sh/1/1
Walker J E	RCAF	81, 243	7+1sh/3/12+3sh	12+1sh/3/12+3sh
Ingalls B J	RCAF	72, 417	7+1sh/-/2	7+1sh/-/2
Chambers H W	RNZAF	154, 242	7/-/1	7+1sh/-/1
Doherty E S	RNZAF	242, 92	7/-/1	7/-/1
Chisholm W L	RCAF	92	6+1sh/3/3	6+2sh/4/4
Curry J H	RCAF (US)	601, 80	6+1sh/2/3	7+1sh/2/3
Jones N G	RAF	152	6+1sh/-/-	6+1sh/-/-
Nicholls J H	RAF	601, 92	5+2sh/2/3	5+2sh/2/3
Livingstone D F	RNZAF	154, 111	5+2sh/-/-	5+2sh/-/-
Samouelle C J	RAF	92	6/4/5	10/4/9
Whitamore W M	RAF	601, 81	6/2/6	10+1sh/3+1sh/11
Hagger R A	RAF	81, 72	6/1/3	7/1/3
Ekbery J S	RAF	232, 145, 93	6/1/1	6/1/1
Andrew J R	RAF	93	6/-/4	6/-/4
Cox G J	RAF	72, 92	6/-/1	8+3sh/1/3+1sh
Fenwick H E	RCAF	81	5+1sh/3+1sh/7	5+1sh/3+1sh/7
Smith L A	RAF	152	5+1sh/1/1	5+1sh/1/2
Morgan J M	RAF	92, 274	5+1sh/1sh/6	7+1sh/1sh/8
Browne S F	RNZAF	93	5+1sh/-/2	5+1sh/-/2
Benham D I	RAF	242	4+2sh/3/7	6+2sh/3/7
Lindsay W R M	RAF	242, 71 OTU Fpln Flt	2+4sh/1/4+1sh	2+4sh/1/4+1sh
Jeandet H	Fr	GC II/7, 326	1+5sh/-/-	2+6sh/-/-
Robinson M E S	SAAF	1 SAAF	5/1/1	5+1sh/1/1
Bunting B	RAAF	93	5/1/1	5/1/1
Kennedy I F	RCAF	111, 93	5/1/-	10+5sh/1/-
Charnock H W	RAF	72	5/1/-	8/1/-
Downer W W	RCAF	93	5/-/2	5/-/2
Askey W M H	RCAF	92	5/-/1	5/-/1
Oxspring R W	RAF	72	4+1sh/1/9	13+2sh/2/13
Mallinson J R	RAF	242	4+1sh/1/1	4+1sh/1/1

Name	Service	Unit/s	Theatre Claims	Total Claims
Banner F S	RAF	243, 145	4+1sh/-/2	5+1sh?/2/2
Griffiths A M	RAF	72	4+1sh/-/3	4+1sh/-/3
McIntosh L	RAAF	111	4+1sh/-/-	4+1sh/-/-
Draper J W P	RCAF	111	4+1sh/2/1	4+1sh/2/1 +6 V1
Montgomerie L J	RNZAF	81, 92	4+1sh/-/2	4+1sh/-/2
Matthews G P H	RAF	145, 111	3+2sh/2/1	6+3sh/2/4+1sh
Smith A	RAF	93	3+2sh/2/1	5+2sh/4/5
Gasson J E	SAAF	92	3+2sh/1/7	3+2sh/1/7
Hardy O L	RNZAF	72	3+2sh/1/4	3+3sh/1/5
Hamblin B W	RAF	242	3+2sh/-/2+2sh	3+2sh/-/2+2sh
Reid W H	RCAF	43	3+2sh/-/-	3+2sh/-/-
Mellor F	RAF	111	2+3sh/1/3	2+3sh/1/3

Aces with some Spitfire Claims in North Africa and Italy

Name	Service	Unit/s	Theatre Claims	Total Claims
Arthur C I R	RAF	232, 72, 5 RFU	1+3sh/-/2	2+4sh/-/2
Bamberger C S	RAF	93, 243	2/-/2	5/1/2
Bartley A C	RAF	111	4/2/1	12+1sh/3/8
Baynham G T	RAF	152	1+2sh/-/-	5+2sh/-/-
Bennetts B R	SAAF	601	2+2sh/-/1	3+2sh/-/1
Bisdee J D	RAF	601, 323 Wg	-/-/1	8+2sh/4/3+1sh
Blanck G	Fr	327/GC I/3	1/-/-	6+6sh/-/-
Boddington M C B	RAF	242	3+1sh/-/-	10+1sh/-/2+1sh
Boillot P	Fr	326/GC II/7	1/-/-	9/-/-
Bosman A C	SAAF	72, 7 SAAF Wg	2/-/-	8+3sh/1/3
Campbell F*	RAF	93	1/2/4+1sh	4/2/6+1sh
Carlson D C	RAF	154, 32	1/-/-	3+2sh/2/1
Conrad W A G	RCAF	145	-/-/1sh	5+3sh/3/10+2sh
Cooper-Slipper T P M	RAF	103 MU	-/-/1	10+2sh/-/4
Cox D G S R	RAF	72	4/3/4	7+1sh/6/5
Cronin L F M	RAAF	81	3/-/3	5/-/5
Daddo-Langlois W R	RAF	93	1/-/-	5½/-/2
Dicks-Sherwood E S	RAF	94, 145, 92	1/-/-	5+2sh/-/5+1sh
Doudies J	Fr	326/GC II/7	2sh/-/-	1+6sh/-/-
Doyle J J	RCAF	417	1/1/-	5/1/4
Dugoujon J	Fr	327/GC 1/3	1/-/-	2+4sh/-/-
Duncan-Smith W G G	RAF	244 Wg, 324 Wg	3/-/2	17+2sh/6+2sh/8
Dundas H S L	RAF	324 Wg	1+2sh/-/-	4+6dh/2sh/2+1sh
Duval R	Fr	327/GC I/3	1/-/-	2+8sh/-/-
Eckford A F	RAF	154, 242	1+2sh/-/-	9+3sh/2/5
Edwards J F	RCAF	417, 92, 274	3/-/2	15+3sh/8+1sh/13
Everard H J	RCAF	417	2/2/2	5+1sh/3/3
Faure J M	SAAF	92, 4 SAAF, 1 SAAF, 324 Wg	2+1sh/-/1	5+1sh/1/1
Foskett R G	RAAF	94	1/-/1	6+1sh/-/5
Gauthier G	Fr	326/GC II/7	1+2sh/-/-	3+7sh/-/-
Gaynor J H	SAAF	1 SAAF, 2 SAAF, 7 SAAF	2+1sh/-/2	5+1sh/-/6
Genders G E C	RAF	103 MU	1+1sh/-/2sh	8+2sh/2/3+2sh
Gilmour W M	RAF	111	2/1/-	9/3/3
Gleed I R	RAF	244 Wg	1/-/2	13+3sh/4+3sh/4
Glendinning A*	RAAF	92	1/-/-	3+2sh/2/2
Gordon D C	RCAF	9 SAAF, 601, 417	1/2/2	9+2sh/5/5
Graham M	RAF	243	1+2sh/-/1	4+2sh/1/3
Hards M H	RAF	601, 92, 111	-/1/-	7/2/4
Harrison G A	RAF	154	2+2sh/1sh/-	3+2sh/1sh/-
Horricks G E	RCAF	417	2/-/-	7+2sh/1sh/6
Jonsson T E	Iceland	111	4/1/-	8/1/2
Jowsey M E	RCAF	92	4/-/2	5/1/3
Krol W S	Pol	145 PFT	4/-/-	8+1sh/1/1sh

Name	Service	Unit/s		
Le Cheminant J	RAF	72, 232	3/-/2	5/1/2
Le Roux J J	RAF	111	4/1/2	18/2/8
Lovell A D J	RAF	322 Wg	3/-/1	16+6sh/2/9+4sh
Marples R	RAF	145	1/-/-	2+5sh/4/3
Metelerkamp P C R	SAAF	1 SAAF	1/-/1	5/-/4
Morris E J	RAF	251 Wg	1+2sh/-/-	2+5sh/1/3
Nelson-Edwards G H	RAF	93	1+1sh/-/6	1+4sh/3+1sh/8
Olver P	RAF	1 SAAF, 244 Wg	3+1sh/-/2	4+2sh/3+1sh/4+2sh
Osler M S	SAAF	145, 601	2+1sh/-/-	9+1sh/-/2
Overton C N	RAF	145	1/-/1	5+1sh/1/1+1sh
Parrott P L	RAF	72, 111, 43	2sh/-/1	5+4sh/-/5+2sh
Peart A M	RNZAF	81	3+1sh/-/4	6+1sh/-/9
Pissotte G	Fr	327/GC I/3	1/-/-	2+6sh/-/-
Popek M	Pol	145 PFT	2/-/1	3+2sh/-/2
Powers MacA	RAF	145	2+1sh/-/1+1sh	7+1sh/-/1+1sh
Rathwell D W	RCAF	81	1+2sh/1sh/-	3+2sh/1sh/3
Rebiere R	Fr	328/GC I/7	1/-/-	4+3sh/-/-
Robertson R J H	RAF	72	3+1sh/-/1	5+1sh/1/3+1sh
Sabourin J J J P	RCAF	145	3+1sh/-/1	6+1sh/-/4
Saphir J	RCAF	417	1/-/-	3+2sh/-/-
Saunders C H	RAF	145	2/2/1	5+2sh/3/3
Savage T W	RAF	92	4/-/2	4+1sh/-/2
Schrader W E	RNZAF	1435	2+1sh/-/-	11+2sh/-/-
Sewell W R P	RCAF	601, 145, 81	3+1sh/2/1	4+1sh/2/2+1sh
Sing J E J	RAF	152	-/-/1	7½/2/2+1sh
Sizer W M	RAF	152, 93	1/1/6+1sh	7+6sh/1/9+1sh
Skalski S	Pol	145 PFT, 601	3/-/1	18+3sh/2/4+1sh
Sporny K	Pol	145 PFT	3/-/-	5/1/1
Sztramko K	Pol	145 PFT	3/-/-	4+1sh/-/-
Thompson P D	RAF	601	2 dest on gnd	2+3sh/1/3
Turner P S	RCAF	417, 244 Wg	-/-/2	10+1sh/1/8
Usher D C	RAF	145	4/-/2	5/-/3
Valentin G	Fr	326/GC II/7	1+1sh/-/-	3+7sh/-/-
van Vliet C A*	SAAF	4 SAAF, 7 SAAF	1/-/-	4/-/- + 8 dest on gnd
Waddy J L	RAAF	92	3/-/2	15+1sh/7/6
Waugh L R S	SAAF	417, 601	-/-/1	6/2/4
West J G	RNZAF	103 MU, 80	1/-/1	4+2sh/1sh/3+1sh
Westenra D F	RNZAF	601, 93	1+1sh/1/1	8+3sh/2/4
Wilmot L A	SAAF	322 Wg, 239 Wg	1/-/-	4+1sh/-/-
Wilson A F	RAF	103 MU, 145, 154	3+1sh/1/2	4+1sh/1/3
Winskill A L	RAF	232	1+1sh/-/1	4+2sh/1/1
			+2/-/2 dest on gnd	+2/-/2 dest on gnd
Woods E N	RAF	249, 286 Wg	1/-/-	11+2sh/4/9

Aces who flew Spitfires in North Africa and Italy but made no Claims

Name	Service	Unit/s	Total Claims
Ashton J H*	RAF	73	4+1unc
Bartlett L H	RAF	253	3+2sh/2+1sh/-
Bary R E	RAF	80, 244 Wg	2+4sh/2/2
Beresford T B de la P	RAF	324 Wg	3+2sh/-/1
Boyd A H	RAF	281 Wg	15+3sh/2/4
Boyle B J L	SAAF	4 SAAF	5+1sh/-/-
Broadhurst H	RAF	AOC WDAF	13/7/10
Carpenter J M V	RAF	417, 92, 145, 72	8/1/3
Clowes A V	RAF	601, 94	9+1sh/3/2
Cochrane H P	RAF	238	7/2/1
Cock J R	RAF	72	10+1sh/4/5
Collingwood R J P	SAAF	152, 81	5/1/1

Dorance M	Fr	328	3+11sh/-/-
du Vivier D A R G L	Belg	239 Wg	3+2sh/1+1sh/1
Ellis R V	RAF	73	3+4sh/-/1
Freeborn J C	RAF	286 Wg	11+2sh/1/1+3sh
Garton G W	RAF	232, 87, 8 SAAF Wg	7+3sh/2/2
Glew N V	RAF	1435	3+3sh/2/6
Golding D W	SAAF	4 SAAF, 73	8+3sh/2/2
Hayter J C F	RNZAF	74	5/1/4
Hugo H	Fr	326	6sh/-/-
Human D W	SAAF	7 SAAF Wg	5/-/+1sh
Joyce E L	RNZAF	73	10/2/3
Kent J A	RAF	17 Sector	12/3/2
Kingcome C B F	RAF	244 Wg	9+3sh/5/13
Laubscher C J	SAAF	242, 10 SAAF, 11 SAAF	4+2sh/2/3
Linton K R	RCAF	417	4+1sh/1/2
Loftus D H	SAAF	7 SAAF Wg	4+1sh/-/3
Madon M	Fr	328	5+6sh/-/-
McBurnie D H	RAAF	451, 238	5+1sh/-/1
Mills J P	RAF	73	3+2sh/-/-
Monraisse M	Fr	328	1+6sh/-/-
Mortimer-Rose E B	RAF	111	9+4sh/3+2sh/5+6sh
Norris S C	RAF	33	8+1sh/1/1+3sh
Ottewill P G	RAF	253	4+2sh/-/1
Plinston G H F	RAF	601	7+1sh/-/-
Proctor J E	RAF	352	9+1sh/1/-
Rook M*	RAF	43	2+1sh/1+1sh/-
Smith F M*	RAF	145	2+1sh/1/1
Sowrey J A	RAF	336	5+2sh/-/1
Swales J O	SAAF	4 SAAF, 10 SAAF	3+2sh/1/2
Thompson J M	RAF	328 Wg	8/1+1sh/7
Villaceque P	Fr	327	1+5sh/-/-
Webb P C	RAF	253	3+3sh/-/5
Wooten E W	RAF	322 Wg	5+1sh/1sh/3
Young M H	RAF	43, 93	7+6sh/-/3

Note

Those pilots with less than five victories are marked thus * and are shown because of their inclusion in *Aces High* or *Those Other Eagles* and where there may be doubt as to their actual scores

— COLOUR PLATES —

1
Spitfire VB AB326/ZX-A of Flt Lt J J P Sabourin, No 145 Sqn, Gambut, Libya, 1 June 1942
As the Battle of Gazala raged, No 145 Sqn flew the first Spitfire operations in the desert on the evening of 1 June 1942 when a pair of aircraft were scrambled. Near Gambut, and flying this aircraft, Flt Lt Joseph Sabourin, in company with Sgt James, intercepted a solitary Ju 88 on a reconnaissance mission and damaged it – the Spitfire's first claim over Egypt. Exactly one week later this same pair shot down a Bf 109 to the southwest of Tobruk to claim the Spitfire's first confirmed victory in North Africa. On 12 June Sabourin shot down Feldwebel Herkenhoff's Bf 109 to become the first pilot to become an ace over Africa whilst flying a Spitfire. This aircraft was lost on operations on 23 June 1942.

2
Spitfire VC ER502/UF-X of Flg Off M R B Ingram, No 601 'County of London' Sqn, El Nogra, Libya, December 1942
New Zealander Flg Off Bruce Ingram had moved with No 601 Sqn to the desert, and by the time ER502 joined the unit in late 1942 he had claimed seven and five shared victories. Finished in desert camouflage, this Spitfire continued the No 601 Sqn convention of adorning its aircraft with the unit's 'winged sword' emblem on the tail. ER502 failed to return from a mission over Tunisia on 16 April 1943.

3
Spitfire VB BR476/QJ-J of Sqn Ldr J H Wedgewood, No 92 Sqn, LG 173, Egypt, August-October 1942
BR476 was the regular aircraft of No 92 Sqn's CO Sqn Ldr Jeff Wedgewood, who claimed the unit's first victory in the

desert whilst flying it on 14 August when he shot down the Bf 109F of Leutnant Mix of II./JG 27. He had also destroyed a C.202 and damaged several Bf 109s with the aircraft by month-end. Wedgewood became an ace flying another Spitfire, but was again in BR476 when he claimed his sixth victory – another Bf 109 – on 2 September. He went on to down four more Messerschmitts with the machine during the heavy fighting of October, taking his total to ten destroyed. Wedgewood's score shown on this aircraft also includes three victories that were claimed by whole formations during the Battle of Britain. Fellow ace Flg Off 'Red' Chisholm also claimed two victories in BR476, which was written off during a take-off accident at Bilbeis, in Egypt, on 11 December 1943. By then the fighter was serving with No 1 Middle East Check and Conversion Unit.

4

Spitfire VC EP193/QJ-U of Flt Lt J L Waddy, No 92 Sqn, LG 173, Egypt, 22 October 1942
Flt Lt John Waddy was one of the leading Australian aces of World War 2, and he had the unusual distinction of flying with RAF, SAAF and RAAF squadrons in both the desert and the Pacific. By the time he joined No 92 Sqn on 3 October he already had 12.5 victories to his name, and it was in this aircraft that he claimed the first of his three Spitfire kills when, over the frontlines at the opening of the Alamein offensive, he shot down a Bf 109F of *JaboGruppe Afrika*. After his distinguished service in Africa, Waddy returned to Australia to become an instructor in early 1943. EP193 saw further operational service in-theatre with Nos 601 and 145 Sqns, however, before being written off in a landing accident at Ismailia, in Egypt, on 23 April 1945 while assigned to No 71 OTU.

5

Spitfire VC EP690/AX-A of Maj P C R Metelerkamp, No 1 Sqn SAAF, LG 05, Egypt, 27 November 1942
No 1 Sqn SAAF began receiving Spitfires in early November 1942, and the unit had its first combats with them on the morning of the 27th. On that date CO, Maj Peter Metelerkamp, flying this aircraft, led ten aircraft into action against eight Bf 109s near Mersa el Brega, one of which he damaged for his squadron's first Spitfire claim. Later on at about 1530 hrs – once more flying EP690/AX-A – he led another patrol that again tangled with Bf 109s (from II./JG 27). Metelerkamp destroyed one of them to claim his fifth victory. Capt Johannes Faure also achieved acedom in the same action. Sadly, on 13 December Metelerkamp was killed by return fire from a bomber. EP690 had been badly damaged in an accident at El Hassiat, in Libya, one week prior to Metelerkamp's death, and following extensive repairs the fighter was issued to No 40 Sqn SAAF. It was subsequently shot down over Sicily on 10 July 1943, resulting in the death of Capt G C le Roux.

6

Spitfire VC ER676/B-E of Flt Lt D I Benham, No 242 Sqn, Bone, Algeria, December 1942
Douglas Benham landed in Algeria with No 242 Sqn soon after the *Torch* invasion and he was quickly in action, making five claims during November – including two shared victories.

At the start of December he began to regularly fly this aircraft, using it on a sweep for the first time on the 2nd and unsuccessfully scrambling after some Ju 88s the next day. Then early on 4 December Benham was at the controls of ER676 on another sweep when some Fw 190s were encountered west of Mateur. In the resulting combat he hit one that was seen to limp away over some hills, and he was credited with a probable. This was Benham's only claim in this aircraft, but he had achieved acedom by early January.

7

Spitfire VC ER220/QJ-R of Flg Off N F Duke, No 92 Sqn, Hamraiet and Wadi Sirru, Libya, January 1943
Having rejoined No 92 Sqn in late 1942, eight-victory ace Flg Off Neville Duke was scrambled from Hamraiet in this aircraft (his regular mount until February 1943) on the morning of 8 January 1943. He and his No 2, Flt Sgt Sales, duly encountered a large formation of Bf 109s and C.202s at 13,000 ft. Diving on a pair of Macchi fighters 3000 ft below them, Duke and Sales chased the Italian aircraft down to ground level. The Spitfire pilots dived almost vertically before Duke managed to hit his target, which broke up and crashed. He was flying ER220 again at lunchtime on the 21st when, near Castel Benito, he met a formation of Ju 87s flying at 1000 ft. As the Stukas dived, Duke got ahead of the formation and fired, hitting one in the starboard wing root and causing it to spin down in flames for his 12th victory. ER220 later served with No 601 Sqn until it was downed by a Bf 110 off Cap Bon on 17 April 1943. Its pilot, Flt Sgt P F Griffiths, took to his parachute and was captured.

8

Spitfire VC ER979/J-J of Sgt F Campbell, No 93 Sqn, Souk el Khemis, Algeria, January-March 1943
On 16 January 1943 ER979 was flown for the first time by future ace Frank Campbell on an escort mission for Hurricane fighter-bombers. It subsequently became the regular mount of Sgt John Humphrey, although Campbell used it for another Hurricane escort on the 22nd. His next flight in it was on 4 March when he helped provide high cover for a Flying Fortress raid on Bizerte. Humphrey, who decorated ER979 with a customised rendition of the Isle of Man coat of arms as well as the name *Marco Polo,* was flying the aircraft on 5 April when his patrol was bounced by 18 Bf 109s. Turning the tables on his attackers, he claimed one German fighter damaged. The next day, once more in ER979, Humphrey shared a probable Bf 109, but on 17 April he was posted missing in this aircraft.

9

Spitfire VB ER773/RS-J of Sqn Ldr S C Norris, No 33 Sqn, Bersis, Libya, February 1943
Nine-victory ace Stan Norris was in the last weeks of his command of Hurricane-equipped No 33 Sqn when the unit received several Spitfire Vs, including ER773, which it retained until May 1943. He took this aircraft aloft for the first time on 2 February, and on the 11th flew it from Benina to Bersis. Norris relinquished his command later that same month, but ER773 remained with No 33 Sqn. It was also regularly flown by another successful pilot, Flt Lt Sandy Kallio, who claimed No 33 Sqn's only Spitfire victory in the desert

when he shot down a Ju 88 on 1 May, albeit in another aircraft. ER773 later served with one of the RAF's Greek units (No 336 Sqn), and was duly transferred to the Royal Hellenic Air Force on 25 April 1946.

10

Spitfire VC ER676/HT-E of Flt Lt A F Aikman, No 154 Sqn, Maison Blanche, Algeria, 26 February 1943

Originally with No 242 Sqn (see Profile 6), ER676 had joined No 154 Sqn by February 1943. Here, the Spitfire was flown by several successful pilots including Flt Lt Alan Aikman, who on the morning of 26 February used it to lead an uneventful patrol of Algiers harbour. Another ace who flew the aircraft was Flt Lt 'Shag' Eckford, as did Flg Off Paddy Chambers, who led a patrol over Sedjenane in ER676. The fighter enjoyed success in the hands of Sgt Costain on the evening of 10 April when he damaged a Bf 109 near Beja, although it went missing (possibly shot down by German fighters) whilst escorting US B-25s sent to attack Tunis 15 days later, with the loss of Sgt J Sillitoe.

11

Spitfire IX EN116/RN-A of Sqn Ldr R W Oxspring, No 72 Sqn, Souk el Khemis, Algeria, March-April 1943

On 1 March 1943 No 72 Sqn's CO, Sqn Ldr Bobby Oxspring, was flying this aircraft in the Beja area when he led his section to support No 152 Sqn. The latter had been engaged by Bf 109s, and boring in he opened fire. 'I let fly and white glycol streamed from the engine as the canopy peeled away and the pilot bailed out'. Unfortunately, the German pilot fell out of his parachute. This was Oxspring's regular aircraft at the time, although this was his only success in it. However, EN116 gained a further victory with an ace on 19 April when, in a sweep over Tunis, Bf 109s were engaged and Flt Lt 'Dan' Daniel destroyed one. He then collided with a second German fighter and had to force land at Oued Zarga.

12

Spitfire VC ER228/ZX-S of Flt Lt J S Taylor, No 145 Sqn, Ben Gardane, Tunisia, 7 March 1943

John Taylor was one of the leading Spitfire pilots of the desert war, having 'made ace' by the end of February 1943. He boosted his score on 1 March when he shot down a Bf 109. Then on the 7th, while flying this aircraft, Taylor was part of a patrol that crossed the frontline at 14,000 ft to the northwest of Medenine. There, they spotted a formation of Bf 109s and C.202s, and Taylor chased one of the latter out over the sea, firing until the fighter came down in the water for his eighth victory. As shown here, by this stage in the war some units (including No 145 Sqn) wore coloured unit code letters outlined in white in contravention to RAF regulations. A long-serving machine, ER228 subsequently spent time with Nos 73 and 253 Sqns prior to being relegated to No 73 OTU. It was written off with the latter unit on 20 July 1945 when its engine cut on take-off from Fayid. The pilot successfully force-landed the fighter.

13

Spitfire IX EN298/RN-B of Flt Lt D G S R Cox, No 72 Sqn, Souk el Khemis, Algeria, March-April 1943

One of the first Spitfire IXs delivered to No 72 Sqn, EN298 was the regular mount of eight-victory ace Flt Lt David Cox during the latter part of the Tunisian campaign. He first flew it in action on 28 February 1943, and continued to fly the aircraft regularly through March. Late on the morning of the 26th, when providing cover to an A-20 raid, Cox used EN298 to damage a Bf 109 over Djebel Tebaga. On the afternoon of 3 April he was again flying the aircraft in the escort role (this time for B-25s attacking Zaghouan) when, on the return flight, Bf 109s were sighted. One of those duly fell to Cox's guns for his final victory – he also damaged a second Messerschmitt. On the evening of the 12th he probably destroyed an Fw 190 to the south of Djebebina in EN298, while his final claim in North Africe came during a sweep on the 19th when Cox damaged a Bf 109 in EN294. By this stage in the war No 72 Sqn wore red unit code letters. EN298 was shot down by Oberleutnant Leo Potjans of 6./JG 53 on 20 June 1943 over Biscari, its pilot, Australian Flg Off Gordon Sharp, being killed.

14

Spitfire VC JK101/FT-Z of Sqn Ldr M Rook, No 43 Sqn, Jemappes, Algeria, April 1943

One of the tallest pilots in the RAF, 'Mickey' Rook had been given command of No 43 Sqn following his service in Russia. Leading the unit out to North Africa in November 1942, he remained in command throughout the Tunisian campaign. Rook had JK101 as his personal mount for much of the time after No 43 Sqn had received Spitfires in February 1943. JK101 later transferred to No 249 Sqn, and like Rook it survived the war.

15

Spitfire IX EN315/ZX-6 of Flt Lt E Horbaczewski, No 145 Sqn Polish Fighting Team, La Fouconnerie, Tunisia, April 1943

One of the most publicised units to fly Spitfires in the desert was the so-called 'Polish Fighting Team' that was embedded within No 145 Sqn. It was irreverently nicknamed 'Skalski's Circus' after its commander. As shown here, the unit's Spitfire IXs wore individual code numbers in place of letters, and were also adorned with the red/white Polish national insignia just forward of the cockpit. The PFT's most successful pilot was Flt Lt Lugeniusz Horbaczewski, who regularly flew EN315 and claimed three victories whilst flying it, including a pair of Bf 109s off the Tunisian coast on 22 April. It is shown here carrying his score before that event Sqn Ldr Stanislaw Skalski also claimed one of his victories at the controls of this machine. Later transferred to No 1 Sqn SAAF, EN315 was written off on 10 July 1943 when its engine cut on take-off from Luqa airfield, Malta, and the fighter hit rocks when its pilot overshot while attempting an emergency landing.

16

Spitfire VC ER807/SN-E of Sqn Ldr J E Walker, No 243 Sqn, Souk el Khemis, Algeria, 10 April 1943

Having become an ace flying with No 81 Sqn in February 1943, James Walker assumed command of No 243 Sqn that same month. Continuing to add to his score, he achieved victories in a variety of aircraft, including ER807. On the evening of 10 April Walker led a sweep in the aircraft over Medjez el Bab at 20,000 ft. Spotting four Bf 109s below him, he led his unit in the perfect bounce. Opening fire on a Messerschmitt, he set it on fire and then the fighter blew up. Switching to another Bf 109, he hit that too and was credited with a damaged. Unlike other units, No 243 Sqn chose not to 'customise' the letter codes applied to its aircraft. ER807 did not survive long, being shot down by Unteroffizier Büsen of III./JG 27 on 8 May off Cap Bon. Its pilot, Plt Off Gordon McKay, was killed. Moments prior to his demise, Canadian McKay had downed a Bf 109, this victory following claims for a Ju 87 destroyed and a second dive-bomber probably destroyed in ER807 on 7 April.

17

Spitfire VC JG871/L-E of Sgt L A Smith, No 152 Sqn, Setif, Algeria, 14 and 21 April 1943
JG871 was a long serving aircraft with No 152 Sqn, and it was flown by several successful pilots including future ace Sgt Len Smith. Indeed, he was at its controls on 14 April when he escorted Hurricane fighter-bombers – a sortie that he repeated in JG871 a week later when the Hurricanes attacked targets near Bizerte. Smith made his first claim soon afterwards. Another ace to fly the fighter was Flt Lt Geoffrey Baynham, who, on 27 April, led the escort for an attack on Pont du Fahs. As depicted here, No 152 Sqn, like a number of Spitfire units in-theatre, applied a single letter unit code (L in this case) to its Spitfires for much of the Tunisian campaign. However, by the time Baynham flew JG871 on a patrol over Sicily on 30 August the squadron had reverted to the more familiar UM codes. The aircraft subsequently served with Nos 154, 73, 32 and 352 Sqns prior to being written off on 13 July 1943 when it hit an obstruction on landing at Misurata West, in Libya.

18

Spitfire IX EN204/FL-L of Sgt L A Cronin, No 81 Sqn, Souk el Khemis and Protville, Algeria, May 1943
Towards the end of the Tunisian campaign EN204 became the regular mount of future Australian ace Larry Cronin. Previously identified as FL-E, the overpainting is evident in this view. Several other notable pilots achieved some success at the controls of EN204 too, Sgt Don Rathwell making his first claim in it (for a Bf 109 probable) on 2 March and Cronin's great friend New Zealander Alan Peart achieving his second victory (also a Bf 109) with the aircraft near Medjez el Bab on 25 April. The next day Flt Lt Bill Olmstead damaged another Messerschmitt whilst flying EN204. Finally, on 28 April Plt Off William Caldecott claimed the second of his four victories in the aircraft when he shared in the destruction of yet another Bf 109. EN204 was written off on 10 June 1943 when it swung on take-off and hit a truck at Takali.

19

Spitfire VC JG839/EY-S of Sqn Ldr R E Bary, No 80 Sqn, Idku, Egypt, 23 May 1943
In April 1943 No 80 Sqn, led by New Zealand ace Sqn Ldr Ron Bary, began re-equipping with Spitfires – the CO made his first flight in one on the 14th. His regular aircraft until he left the unit in July was ER872, but in the early afternoon of 23 May Bary flew several practice intercepts in JG839. For some reason this particular aircraft wore red unit letters, although other Spitfires in the squadron wore regulation

white. Bary was promoted to wing commander and left No 80 Sqn soon afterwards. It was not until late July that the unit at last claimed its first Spitfire successes when two Ju 88s were shot down. Based in Egypt, however, No 80 Sqn saw little further action with the aircraft. JG839 later served with No 10 Sqn SAAF and 94 Sqns.

20

Spitfire IX MA408/CG of Wg Cdr C F Gray, No 322 Wing, Lentini East, Sicily, August 1943
The leading New Zealand fighter pilot of World War 2 in terms of aerial victories, Colin Gray commanded No 322 Wing throughout the Sicily campaign. He flew his first personally marked Spitfire, EN350, during this period, although the aircraft was replaced by MA408 some time in late July. Gray used the latter aircraft for the remainder of his tour, which concluded in early September. Wearing standard desert camouflage, the fighter has been adorned with Gray's initials in non-standard colours, just like those adopted by some of the squadrons under his command. Gray returned to England, while MA408 served with Nos 74, 73 and 253 Sqns of the BAF prior to being scrapped in June 1948.

21

Spitfire VC JK322/FL-4 of Flg Off A M Peart, No 81 Sqn, Takali, Malta, 16 July 1943
JK322 was one of a number of Spitfire Vs issued to 81 Sqn when it had to pass some Spitfire IXs onto other units. To differentiate between the marks, the squadron applied numbers in place of individal aircraft letters, and JK322 also bore the name *JOY* beneath its cockpit. Future ace Flg Off Alan Peart made his first claim over Sicily when, on 16 July, he damaged a Bf 109 while flying JK322 over Catania. Nine days later Plt Off Wiliam Caldecott shot down a Ju 52/3m with it. JK322, which wears the coloured unit codes used by some units, did not survive long, for the aircraft was destroyed in an air raid on the Sicilian airfield of Lentini on the night of 12 August 1943.

22

Spitfire IX JK980 of Flt Lt J G West, No 103 MU attached to No 94 Sqn, Savoia, Libya, 24 August 1943
To counter enemy high altitude reconnaissance flights over Egypt, No 103 MU at Aboukir had a high altitude flight equipped with specially modified Spitfires. These machines were occasionally detached to operate alongside frontline units, such as in early August 1943 when New Zealand ace Flt Lt 'Shorty' West took some aircraft (including JK980) to Savoia to fly with Spitfire VC-equipped No 94 Sqn. On the 13th he was scrambled and damaged a Bf 109G over the Nile Delta area. After several further scrambles, on the 24th West took off in this aircraft and intercepted another Bf 109G at high altitude. This time he managed to shoot the aircraft down, giving him his sixth, and final, victory. JK980, seen here finished in a highly polished high altitude colour scheme, was also flown by No 94 Sqn pilots, including the unit's ace CO, Sqn Ldr 'Darky' Clowes. Converted from a Spitfire VC into a Mk IX on the Castle Bromwich production line in the spring of 1943, JK980 later served with Nos 74 and 451 Sqns and was eventually transferred to the *Armée de l'Air* in June 1946.

23

Spitfire IX MA454/UM-V of Flt Lt G T Baynham, No 152 Sqn, Lentini East, Sicily, 27 August 1943

Transferred in from No 111 Sqn, this aircraft was the usual mount of Flg Off R J Bell. Like other Spitfire IXs flown by No 152 Sqn in the summer of 1943, it had prominent black unit codes – probably to distinguish them from the Mk Vs also in use by the unit. Among several aces in the squadron at this time was Flt Lt Geoffrey Baynham, who had achieved this distinction on 25 July 1943. On the morning of 27 August he flew MA454 on a low-level convoy escort off the Sicilian coast. This was possibly the only operational mission he logged in the aircraft. A month later, on 25 September, fellow ace and No 322 Wing Leader Lt Col Laurie Wilmot flew the Spitfire on a freelance anti-Ju 52/3m patrol. MA454 was later transferred to No 1 Sqn SAAF, and on 20 February 1945 it force-landed in neutral Switzerland after being hit by flak over Udine, in northern Italy.

24

Spitfire IX LZ950/EF-F of Flt Lt W A Olmstead, No 232 Sqn, Montecorvino, Sicily, 11 and 24 September 1943

Unlike most other Spitfire units in the Mediterranean area, No 232 Sqn broadly adhered to the official style of markings, as shown on LZ950. This aircraft was flown several times by one of the unit's notable pilots, Flt Lt Bill Olmstead, who on 11 September was airborne in it over the Salerno beaches. During the patrol a formation of German fighter-bombers approached, and in the subsequent engagement over Benevento he damaged a Bf 109. Olmstead flew LZ950 again over Salerno later in the month. The aircraft remained with No 232 Sqn until it crashed in poor weather southeast of Kambla, in Cyprus, on 29 January 1944.

25

Spitfire VC ER863 '7' of Cdt H Hugo. *Groupe de Chasse* **II/7, Ajaccio, Corsica, October 1943**

Following the *Torch* landings in North Africa, the former Vichy French units were incorporated into the Allied command and re-equipped. One was GC II/7, which during the summer of 1943 was re-equipped with Spitfires and committed to operations over the Mediterranean. GC II/7 was led by Cdt Henri Hugo, who had been credited with six shared victories during 1940. Under him it participated in the liberation of Corsica, the unit subsequently flying from the island. The French squadrons adapted the RAF roundels to French colours, and some also wore unit markings, as shown here. On 1 December GC II/7 was re-designated No 326 Sqn in RAF parlance. ER863 subsequently served with No 208 Sqn until it was lost near the Italian town of Rieti during an armed reconnaissance mission on 6 June 1944.

26

Spitfire IX EN459/HN-D of Flt Lt I F Kennedy, No 93 Sqn, Tortorolla, Italy, 15 October 1943

When he joined No 93 Sqn as a flight commander in mid-September, Canadian 'Hap' Kennedy already had five and five shared victories to his name. He continued his run of success with this new unit, claiming three more kills. The last of these came on 15 October 1943 in this aircraft when, covering the American advance across the Volturno River, he became

involved in a dogfight over Sparanise that eventually resulted in him claiming a Bf 109G for his 13th victory. This was his last kill in the Mediterranean, although he achieved further successes over Normandy in 1944. EN459 had previously served with Nos 145 and 601 Sqns prior to being transferred to No 93 Sqn.

27

Spitfire VC JK465/GN-X of Sqn Ldr E N Woods, No 249 Sqn, Grottaglie, Italy, October-November 1943

One of Malta's veteran units, No 249 Sqn moved to Italy in late October 1943. Its CO at this time was Sqn Ldr 'Timber' Woods, an 11-victory ace. JK465 had by then been his regular aircraft for some time, and he continued to use it after the move. Indeed, he led the squadron's first operation (strafing a radar site near Durazzo) in it on 2 November. This mission was followed by bomber escorts and sweeps throughout the month. On 4 December Flt Lt Beatson was flying JK465 when scrambled to the Berat area, where he and his wingman shot down a Ju 52/3m of II./TG 4. At this time No 249 Sqn's aircraft seem to have been painted in a variation of the high altitude scheme, but with full sized unit codes and a rear fuselage band – an unusual combination. JK465 survived the war and was transferred to French control in September 1945.

28

Spitfire VC LZ943/BQ-B of Flg Off D H McBurnie, No 451 Sqn, El Daba, Egypt, 18 November 1943

Don McBurnie became an ace flying Kittyhawks in the desert, and in late 1943 he joined No 451 Sqn just as it was being re-equipped with Spitfire VCs. Based in Egypt, however, there was little prospect of action other than the occasional scramble against a reconnaissance aircraft. Amongst the Spitfires flown by McBurnie at this time was LZ943, which he used to give escort to convoy *Nightingale* off the Egyptian coast on 18 November 1943. McBurnie later commanded a Spitfire squadron in Italy, whilst LZ943 was transferred to No 73 OTU. Passed on to No 2 Ferry Unit, it swung on landing in soft ground and overturned at Larnaca, on Cyprus, on 19 February 1945.

29

Spitfire VB EP751 of Flt Lt W R M Lindsay, Floatplane Flight, No 71 OTU, Fanora, Egypt, December 1943

Intended for possible use from island bases in the Aegean, three Spitfire VB floatplanes were shipped out to Egypt and delivered to No 71 OTU. The unit duly established a Floatplane Flight at Fanora, on the Great Bitter Lake, under the command of Flt Lt Willie Lindsay – a six-victory Spitfire ace with No 242 Sqn during the Tunisian campaign. Only two of the aircraft (EP751 and EP754) were actually assembled, and on 2 December Lindsay made the first Spitfire floatplane sortie when he eased EP751 off the waters of the lake for a familiarisation flight. The remaining four pilots also soon got airborne, and both fighters were flown regularly until the planned operational deployment was cancelled in mid-December. Lindsay flew his last sortie in this aircraft on 13 December, when he practised formation flying and water landings. EP751 was struck off charge in the Middle East on 28 December 1944.

30

Spitfire VIII JF627/AN-M of Flg Off G E Horricks, No 417 Sqn, Canne, Italy, 9 January 1944

After achieving acedom flying over Malta during 1942, Canadian Garth Horricks joined the only RCAF fighter squadron in the Mediterranean in mid-1943 and claimed his first success with the unit on 8 December. Much of No 417 Sqn's activities during this period centred on ground attack missions, and on 9 January 1944 he flew this aircraft on an offensive patrol – led by his ace CO, Sqn Ldr Bert Houle – that saw a number of locomotives strafed. Just over a month later Horricks claimed his ninth, and final, victory when he shot down an Fw 190 in the Anzio area. He was declared tour expired soon afterwards. JF627 had served with Nos 92 and 208 Sqns prior to joining No 417 Sqn, and it ended the conflict back at No 92 Sqn.

31

Spitfire VIII JF476/QJ-D of Lt J H Gasson, No 92 Sqn, Marcianise, Italy, 16 February 1944

SAAF pilot John Gasson joined No 92 Sqn during the Sicily campaign, and he remained with the unit until 1945, eventually rising to command it. On 16 February 1944 he was flying this aircraft near Rome when his patrol ran into a gaggle of Fw 190s and Bf 109s. Several of the German fighters were shot down, including a Bf 109 that was credited to Gasson as his second victory – it also took No 92 Sqn's total of aircraft destroyed to 300! Gasson achieved his fifth success on St George's Day, 23 April. No 92 Sqn aircraft continued to wear red unit codes and the cobra badge in a white triangle on the nose through to VE Day. Although delivered new to No 92 Sqn, JF476 had spent time with No 145 Sqn before being returned to No 92 Sqn in early 1944. It suffered an in-flight engine failure just days after Gasson claimed his victory on 16 February, the pilot being forced to bail out off Felice Point.

32

Spitfire IX MH660/V-Y of Flt Lt W E Schrader, No 1435 Sqn, Brindisi, Italy, 4 March 1944

After distinguished service in Malta, No 1435 Sqn later moved to Italy. Among its pilots at this time was New Zealander Warren Schrader, who began his path to acedom with the unit. MH660 joined No 1435 Sqn in early 1944, and on the morning of 4 March it was flown by Schrader on a weather check to the Gulf of Kotor in poor conditions. He flew it again several times in March shortly before he left for England. MH660 wore a small unit badge on the fin and bore a distinctive dragon's head as a personal marking beneath the cockpit. MH660 remained with the squadron until it suffered an engine fire and crashed into the Adriatic near Vis on 7 September 1944.

33

Spitfire IX MA766/GO-F of Sqn Ldr R G Foskett, No 94 Sqn, Bu Amud, Egypt, 6 June 1944

No 94 Sqn's Australian CO Sqn Ldr Russ Foskett was flying MA766 on 6 June 1944 when he claimed his seventh, and last, victory by forcing a Ju 52/3m to land at Tmimi, where it was captured. His squadron was involved in operations across the Mediterranean, primarily escorting fighter-bombers. Its Spitfires wore a variety of colour schemes, with MA766 being finished in 'high altitude' colours, although with otherwise standard markings. Note that it is also missing its canopy, pilots dispensing with these for several low-level Beaufighter escort missions in an attempt to keep cool in the cockpit. They were quickly reinstated, however, because of wind buffeting and excessive engine noise! Foskett always had aircraft 'F' as his personal mount, and he flew MA766 during May and June. It was written off in an accident on 7 July 1944.

34

Spitfire IX PL348/TM of Wg Cdr E J Morris, No 251 Wing, Cuers, France, September 1944

Like many other wing leaders, Wg Cdr 'Teddy' Morris used the privilege of his position to carry his initials on his personal aircraft. When leading No 251 Wing, the South African-born ace initially used MK187, in which he achieved his final two victories. When it was withdrawn, the fighter was replaced by this aircraft, PL348, which became the new 'TM'. It was regularly flown on operations by Morris, such as on 15 September when he led No 451 Sqn on an armed reconnaissance over northern Italy. He continued to fly it until he was posted at the end of 1944. PL348 was written off in a landing accident at Iesi, in Italy, on 8 September 1945.

35

Spitfire IX MJ250/UF-Q of Flt Lt D Ibbotson, No 601 'County of London' Sqn, Fano, Italy, July-November 1944

Unlike its contemporaries in No 601 Sqn, MJ250 sported a natural polished metal finish in place of the more normal camouflage, possibly as a trial. Among the pilots to fly it regularly on the unit's hazardous fighter-bomber missions was Flt Lt Desmond Ibbotson, who was an ace with 11 victories, nine of them flying Spitfires over the desert and Italy. He returned for a second tour with No 601 Sqn during early 1944 and became a flight commander, flying MJ250 from July. However, on 19 November he was killed in a flying accident in another aircraft, while MJ250 was scrapped in June 1945.

36

Spitfire VIII JF880/AN-U of Flt Lt K R Linton, No 417 Sqn, Bellaria, Italy, 14 March 1945

Karl Linton became an ace flying on sweeps from England during 1943, and after a rest tour he joined No 417 Sqn in Italy in early 1945. By this stage of the war the enemy had been all but swept from Italian skies, so the squadron concentrated on ground attack missions. The five-victory ace flew his first sortie on 22 February when 12 aircraft bombed Meola railway bridge. Linton subsequently led similar missions, and on 14 March he was at the controls of this aircraft when he led four aircraft as escorts for a pair of tactical reconnaissance aircraft overflying the frontline. JF880 had served with the USAAF and No 145 Sqn prior to joining No 417 Sqn, and it was subsequently passed on to No 92 Sqn. The fighter was struck off charge in March 1946.

Back Cover Photograph

A gaggle of Spitfire VCs from No 417 Sqn RCAF patrol over Tunisia in April 1943, a few weeks before the German surrender (*Canadian Forces*)

BIBLIOGRAPHY

Avery, Max and Shores, Christopher, *Spitfire Leader.* Grub St, 1997

Beale, Nick et al, *Air War Italy 1944-45.* Airlife, 1996

Bowyer, Michael, *Fighting Colours.* PSL, 1969 and 1975

Cull, Brian, *249 at War.* Grub St, 1997

Cull, Brian et al, *Spitfires over Sicily.* Grub St, 2000

Flintham, Vic and Thomas, Andrew, *Combat Codes.* Airlife, 2003 and 2008

Franks, Norman, *The War Diaries of Neville Duke.* Grub St, 1995

Griffin, John and Kostenuk, Samuel, *RCAF Squadron Histories and Aircraft.* Stevens, 1977

Halley, James, *Squadrons of the RAF and Commonwealth.* Air Britain, 1988

Herrington, John, *Australians in the War 1939-45, Series 3 Volume 3.* Halstead Press, 1962

Hunt, Leslie, *Twenty One Squadrons.* Garnstone Press, 1972

Jefford, Wg Cdr C G, *RAF Squadrons.* Airlife, 1988 and 2001

Jonsson, Tony, *Dancing the Skies.* Grub St, 1994

Leeson, Frank, *The Hornet Strikes (213 Sqn).* Air Britain, 1998

Louw, Martin and Bouwer, Stefaan, *The SAAF at War.* van Rensburg Pubs, 1995

McLean, Steven, *Squadrons of the SAAF 1920-2005.* Private, 2005

Milberry, Larry and Halliday, Hugh, *The RCAF at War 1939-1945.* CANAV Books, 1990

Minterne, Don, *73 Squadron Part 3.* Tutor Publications, 2000

Oxspring, Gp Capt Bobby, *Spitfire Command.* William Kimber, 1984

Peart, Alan McGregor, *North Africa to the Arakan.* Grub St, 2008

Rawlings, John D R, *Fighter Squadrons of the RAF.* Macdonald, 1969

Richards, Denis, *RAF Official History 1939-45, Parts 2 and 3.* HMSO, 1954

Robertson, Bruce, *Spitfire - The story of a Famous Fighter.* Harleyford, 1960

Shacklock, P, *Eric Genders - Fighter Ace and Test Pilot.* HPM, 1998

Shores, Christopher et al, *Fighters over the Desert.* Neville Spearman, 1969

Shores, Christopher et al, *Fighters over Tunisia.* Neville Spearman, 1971

Shores, Christopher, *Those Other Eagles.* Grub St, 2004

Shores, Christopher and Williams, Clive, *Aces High Vol 1.* Grub St, 1994

Shores, Christopher, *Aces High Vol 2.* Grub St, 1999

Sturtivant, Ray et al, *Spitfire International.* Air Britain, 2002

ACKNOWLEDGEMENTS

The author wishes to record his gratitude to the following who have given of their time in presenting accounts or information for inclusion within this volume – the late Wg Cdr J M V Carpenter DFC, Sqn Ldr D A S Colvin DFC, the late AVM C W Coulthard CB CBE DFC, the late Wg Cdr D S G R Cox DFC and bar, Larry Cronin (son of the late Flt Lt L Cronin DFC), the late Sqn Ldr N F Duke DSO OBE DFC, Wg Cdr J F Edwards DFC and bar DFM CD, Wg Cdr O L Hardy, the late Flt Lt W R M Lindsay, Sqn Ldr H H Moon, Flt Lt A McG Peart DFC, Frank Twitchett Esq., the late A J Watton Esq., the late Air Cdre Sir Archie Winskill KCVO CBE DFC and bar, and the late Air Cdre E W Wooten CBE DFC and bar AFC.

INDEX

References to illustrations are shown in **bold**. Plates are shown with page and caption locators in brackets.

Afrika Korps 7, 10, 12, 14, 31
Aikman, Flt Lt Alan F **27**, 27, **28**, **10**(40, 91), 54
Andrew, Flt Sgt James 52, **66**, 66–67, 71
Arthur, Sqn Ldr 'Duke' **72**, 72, 73, 75, 77
Ashton, Sqn Ldr J H 85
Aspinal, Flt Sgt J T **72**, 73

Bamberger, Flt Lt Cyril 53, 74
Bartley, Sqn Ldr Tony 26, 30
Bary, Wg Cdr Ron E **37**, **19**(42, 92), 77, **83**, 83
Baynham, Flt Lt Geoffrey T **23**(43, 93), 56, 92

Benham, Flt Lt Douglas I **24**, 24, 29–30, **6**(39, 90)
Berry, Sqn Ldr 'Ras' 23, 24, 26, 31
Bird, Sgt Jeff 'Dickie' **72**, 73
Blackburn, Flt Lt Basil **72**, 72–73
Blanck, Lt Georges 61–62
Boddington, Sqn Ldr Mike **50**, 50
Brebner, Capt Don M **4**, 22, 77
British Army: 8th Army 10, 14, 16, 19, 21, 49, 56, 73, 74, 76, 85; 51st Highland Division 19; New Zealand Division/Corps 14, 21
Browne, Flg Off Stan 33–34, 50, 51, 52
Bunting, WO Bobby **68**, 69, 70, 75
Burl, Lt Ray 78
Butler, Flt Sgt **81**, 82

Campbell, Sgt Francis **25**, **8**(39, 90)
Canadian Air Force, Royal: No 417 Sqn 17, 20, 21, **30**(45, 94), **36**(46, 94), 47, 53, 62, 64, 65, 66, **67**, 67, **94**
Carlson, Sqn Ldr Don 24, 27
Chambers, Flg Off 'Paddy' 27, 91
Charnock, WO 'Chas' 29
Chisholm, Flg Off 'Red' **11**, 11, 15, 90
Colvin, Flt Lt Derek 81, 82
Cooper-Slipper, Flt Lt Mike 13, 36–37
Coulthard, Flg Off Colin 50
Cox, Flt Lt David G S R 27, **32**, 32, **13**(41, 91)
Cox, Sqn Ldr Graham **68**, 68, 74, 75
Crafts, Flg Off H A 'Joe' 23
Cronin, WO Larry A 26, **36**, **18**(42, 92), 56

Daddo-Langlois, Flt Lt Raoul 50
Daniel, Sqn Ldr 'Dan' 32, 33, 50–51, 52, 77, 91
Dicks-Sherwood, Flg Off Eric 'Dicky' 17, 49, 56
Doherty, Flt Sgt Eric **56**, 56, 74
Downer, WO Bill 68, 70, 71
Doyle, Plt Off Jack 62, 70–71
Draper, Flg Off Bill 27–28, 30, **31**, 36
Duke, Sqn Ldr Neville **15**, 15, 18, **19**, 19, 21, 34–35, **7**(39, 90), 69, 70, 73, 74, 75, 76–77, 85
Duncan-Smith, Gp Capt Wilf 51, 53, 57, 75
Dundas, Wg Cdr Hugh 'Cocky' 48, 53
Duval, Cne Roger 60–61

Eckford, Flt Lt 'Shag' 24, 91
Edwards, 'Eddie' 68, 69
Ekbery, Flg Off Joe S 30, 32, 49, 54, 74
El Alamein, Battle of (1942) 12, 13–16

Faure, Maj Johannes 'Hannes' 15, 55, **66**, 90
Feldzer, Adj Constantin 47
Fenwick, Flg Off Harry 24, 29
Foskett, Sqn Ldr Russ G **33**(46, 94), **79**, 79, 80, **82**, 82
French Air Force, Free: GC I/3 60–61, 62; GC II/7 'Nice' (later RAF No 326 Sqn) 36, 37, **25**(44, 93), 47, **60**, 60, **61**, 62; GC II/7 pilots **60**

Gasson, Maj John H **31**(45, 94), 49, **70**, **71**, 71
Gauthier, Cne Gabrielle 61, 62
Gaynor, Maj Harry 15, 19, **69**, 69
Gazala, Battle of (1942) 6, 7–8
Genders, Plt Off Eric 'Jumbo' **9**, 9, **10**, 11–12, 13
German army: 10th Army 73, 85
Gilroy, Gp Capt 'Sheep' 31, 33, 48, 52, 59
Gleed, Wg Cdr 'Widge' 20, 35
Gray, Wg Cdr Colin F 31, 33, **34**, **20**(42, 92), 47, 48, **55**, 55–56

Hanley, Plt Off Eric 8, 9–10
Hardy, Flt Lt Owen 26, 33
Henderson, Flt Lt 'Hindoo' 70
Hendry, Flg Off R Bruce **72**, 73
Henschel Hs 293 (Fritz-X) radio-guided bomb 59, 60, 61
Hill, Sqn Ldr George 31–32, 48, 51, 52
Horbaczewski, Flt Lt Eugeniusz 22, **34**, **15**(41, 91), 59
Horricks, Flt Sgt T E 'Tony' 24, 25–26, 30
Houle, Sqn Ldr Bert 16, 17–18, 62, 64, 65, 66, 67–68, 94
Hughes, Flg Off Tom 51
Hugo, Cdt Henri **25**(44, 93), **60**, 60
Hugo, Gp Capt Pieter H 'Dutch' 23, 24, 26, 27, 48, 80
Humphrey, Sgt John **25**, 90
Humphreys, Sqn Ldr P H 50
Hussey, Flt Lt Roy 27, **49**, 49, 60, 66

Ibbotson, Flt Lt Desmond 14, 15–16, **35**(46, 94), 69–70, **77**, 77
Ingalls, Flg Off Bruce 51, 68
Ingram, Sqn Ldr M R Bruce **8**, **10**, 10, 12, 16, **2**(38, 89), 60

James, Sgt 6, **7**, 9
Jeandet, Lt Henri 61
Jones, Flg Off Norman 54, 56
Jonsson, Flt Sgt T E 'Tony' **24**, 25–26, 30
Jowsey, Flg Off Milt 19, 49, 51, 53, **57**

Kallio, Flt Lt Sandy **22**, 90–91
Keith, Flg Off George 51, 53, 56
Kennedy, Flt Lt I F 'Hap' **26**(44, 93), 58, 59, **63**, 63
Kingcome, Wg Cdr Brian **47**, 47

Lanham, Lt J R **21**, 21
Le Cheminant, Flg Off 'Chem' 35
Lees, Gp Capt Ronnie 27
Lindsay, Flt Lt Willie R M 24, 28, 29, 33, **29**(45, 93), 79
Linton, Flt Lt Karl R **36**(46, 94)
Lovell, Wg Cdr Tony 75

Mackie, Sqn Ldr Evan 'Rosie' **48**, 48, 52, 53, 63–64, 67, 68
Maguire, Flt Lt William 31, 36, 54, 58, 64
Mallinson, Sgt James 24, 28, 30

Marples, Sqn Ldr Roy 15, 18
Matthews, Sqn Ldr Peter 13, 14, 64
McBurnie, Flt Lt Don H **28**(44, 93), 71–72
McMillan, Richard 49–50, 53–54
Mellor, Flt Sgt Frank 48
Merwe, Lt van der 22, 55
Messerschmitt: Bf 109 **4**, 68; Bf 109F **14**, 17; Me 323 **4**, **35**, 35
Metelerkamp, Maj Peter C R 15, **16**, 16, **5**(39, 90)
Monk, Flt Lt 8, 9
Montgomerie, Flt Lt Leighton 56, 71, 76
Moon, Flt Lt Paddy 67
Morgan, Sqn Ldr John 14, 15, 17, **67**, 67
Morris, Wg Cdr E J 'Teddy' **34**(46, 94), **71**, 71–72, **74**, 74–75

Neumann, Oberst Eduard 85
Norris, Sqn Ldr Stan C **22**, **9**(40, 90–91)

Olmstead, Flt Lt W A 'Bill' **24**(43, 93), 63, 92
Olver, Wg Cdr Peter 16, 19, 35, 47–48, 51
Operation: Dragoon 75; Flax **4**, 33; Supercharge 14; Torch 15, 23–26; Vesuvius 60–62
Osler, Maj Bennie 62, 68
Oxspring, Sqn Ldr R W 'Bobby' 26, 27, 29, **32**, 32, **11**(40, 91)

Parrott, Sqn Ldr Peter 68–69
Pearce, Flg Off Norm 83, 84–85
Peart, Plt Off Alan M 23, 26, 28, 35–36, **36**, **21**(43, 92), **54**, 54, 57, 59
Perrier, Lt Roger 37
Powers, Flt Sgt 'Mac' 13, 15

Rathwell, Sqn Ldr Don 36, 56, 92
Reid, Flg Off Wilmer 64, 65
Reim, Lt M F 77
Robertson, Plt Off 'Robbie' 28, 29
Robinson, Lt 'Robbie' **4**, 19, 22, **35**, 35, 53–54
Robinson, Flt Sgt Win 57
Rogan, Lt Doug **16**, 19
Rommel, GFM Erwin 7, 8, 9, 12, 14, 16, 19, 31, 33
Royal Air Force: Balkan Air Force (BAF) 80–82; Desert Air Force (DAF) 8, 53, 54, 76; Gibraltar Defence Flight 'Gib Flight'/'Y' Sqn (later No 256 Sqn, 'C' Flight) 23, 37; No 71 OTU, Floatplane Flight **29**(45, 93), 79; No 103 MU, High Altitude Flight 9, **10**, 11–12, 13, 17, 36–37, **37**, **22**(43, 92); Western Desert Air Force (WDAF) 6, 13–14, 19–20, 21
Royal Air Force squadrons: No 32: 37, 67, 82; No 33: **22**, **9**(40, 90–91); No 43: 31, **14**(41, 91), 53, 64, 65, 75, **76**; No 72: 24, 26–27, 29, **32**, 32, 33, **11**(40, 91), **13**(41, 91), 51–52, 53, 56, 60, 66, **72**, 72–73, 75; No 72, pilots **72**; No 73: 82, 83, 84–85; No 74: 78; No 80: 7, **37**, **19**(42, 92); No 81: 23, 24, 25, 33, **34**, **36**, **18**(42, 92), **21**(43, 92), **54**, 56, 57, 59, 60; No 92: 6, 7, 10–11, **11**, **12**, 13–14, **15**, 15, 16–17, **18**, 19, 21, 34–35, **3**, **4**(38–89–90), **7**(39, 90), **31**(45, 94), 47, 49, 51, 53, **57**, 58, 63–64, 65, 68, **70**, **71**, 71, 76; No 92, pilots **70**; No 93: 24, **25**, 33–34, **8**(39, 90), **26**(44, 93), 51, 52, **63**, 63, 65, 66, 75; No 94: 17, **33**(46, 94), **79**, 79–80, 82, 83–84, **84** see also No 103 MU, High Altitude Flight; No 111: 24, 25–26, 27, 30, 31–32, 48, 51, 52, 58, **73**, 75; No 145: **6**, 6–8, **7**, 9–10, 13–15, 16–17, **20**, 20, 21, 22, **1**(38, 89), **12**(40, 91), 48, 48, 52, 63, 75; No 145, 'Polish Fighting Team' (PFT) **4**, 21, 22, 33, **34**, **15**(41, 91); No 152: 24, 32, **17**(42, 92), **23**(43, 93), 54–55, **55**, 56, **58**, 60; No 154: 24, 27, 27, 31, **10**(40, 91), 54, 58, 64, 71; No 232: 29, 30, 32–33, 34, **24**(43, 93), 47, 54, 63, 71; No 242: 23, **24**, 24, 29–30, **6**(39, 90), 50, 56, 71, 74; No 242, pilots **50**; No 243: **24**(41, 91–92), **48**, 48, 52, 63, 75; No 249: **27**(44, 93), **80**, 80–81, 82; No 253: 82, **85**; No 256, 'C' Flight (formerly 'Gib Flight') 23, 37; No 274: 11, **67**, 67, 69; No 352: 83; No 451: **28**(44, 93), 71, 74–75; No 601 'County of London' **6**, **8**, 8, 9, **10**, 10, 13–14, 15–17, 18, **2**(38, 89), **35**(46, 94), 52, 53, 62, 69–70, **77**, 83; No 603: **79**, 79; No 1435: **32**(45, 94), **81**, 81–82

Royal Air Force wings: No 244: 10–11, 20, 21, 47–48, 51, 53; No 251: **34**(46, 94), **71**; No 322: 31, **20**(42, 92), 47–48, **55**, 55, 57, 71; No 324: 24, 47–48, 75–76; No 332 (Free French) 62, 75–76; No 337: 82

Sabourin, Flt Lt Joseph J P **6**, 6, **7**–8, 13, **1**(38, 89)
Sachs, Lt Albert 65
Samouelle, Flt Lt 'Sammy' **11**, 11, **13**, 13, 14, 15, 19
Savage, Flt Lt 'Doc' 49
Schalkwyk, Lt Petrus van **72**, 73
Schrader, Flt Lt Warren E **32**(45, 94), **81**, 82
Simmonds, Flg Off Rodney 83–84, **84**
Sizer, Sqn Ldr Wilf 53
Skalski, Sqn Ldr Stanislaw 21, 22, **33**, 33, **34**, 52, 91
Slade, Sqn Ldr Jack/John 82, 83–84
Slessor, AM John 75
Smith, Sgt Len A **17**(42, 92), **55**, 55, 56
South African Air Force (SAAF) 77; No 1 Sqn **4**, 11, 15, **16**, 16–17, 18, 19, 21, 21, 22, **35**, 35, **5**(39, 90), 47, 53, 55, 58, 59, 70, 77; No 2 Sqn **69**, 69; No 4 Sqn 70, 77; No 7 Sqn 78; No 24 Sqn 79
Steinhoff, Maj Johannes 'Macki' 48–49, **56**, 56
Stirling, Flt Sgt Colin 'Jock' 73
Supermarine Spitfire 16, 23
  Spitfire Mk VB 6–7, 17, **22**; AB324 **7**; AB326 **6**, **1**(38, 89); BR114 **10**; BR476 **12**, **3**(38, 89–90); ER773 **9**(40, 90–91); floatplane **29**(45, 93), 79
  Spitfire Mk VC **4**, 32, **69**, 94; BR392 **10**; BR523 **11**; EP193 **4**(38, 90); EP690 **16**, **5**(39, 90); ER171 **35**; ER220 15, 18, **7**(39, 90); ER228 20, **12**(40, 91); ER486 **67**; ER502 **8**, **2**(38, 89); ER676 24, **27**, **6**(39, 90), **10**(40, 91); ER807 **16**(41, 91–92); ER863 **25**(44, 93); 60; ER882 **21**; ER979 **25**, **8**(39, 90); ES252 **20**; ES353 53; JG839 37, **19**(42, 92); JG871 **17**(42, 92); JG959 **4**; JK101 **14**(41, 91); JK322 **21**(43, 92), **54**; JK465 **27**(44, 93), **80**; JK715 48; LZ807 **55**; LZ943 **28**(44, 93); MA289 **58**; MH558 **79**
  Spitfire Mk VIII 62, 64; JF476 **31**(45, 94), **71**; JF627 **30**(45, 94), **67**; JF880 **36**(46, 94); MT648 **70**
  Spitfire Mk IX 21, 31, 32, 56; EN116 **11**(40, 91); EN204 **15**, **18**(42, 92); EN298 **12**, **13**(41, 91); EN315 **15**(41, 91); EN445 **34**; EN459 **34**, **26**(44, 93), **63**; EP813 61; JK980 **37**, **22**(43, 92); LZ950 **24**(43, 93); MA408 **20**(42, 92); MA454 **23**(43, 93); MA485 **85**; MA766 **33**(46, 94); MH660 **32**(45, 94), **81**; MJ250 **35**(46, 94), 77; MJ282 **73**; MJ532 77; MJ730 **84**; MJ778 **85**; MK171 **72**; MT714 **76**; PL348 **34**(46, 94), **71**
Sutton, Flt Lt 70, 74

Taylor, Sqn Ldr John S 9, 10, **18**, 19, **20**, 21, **12**(40, 91), 52
Taylor, Capt Tom **66**, 66
Turkington, Flt Lt 'Paddy' 64, 75

United States Army: 5th Army 63, 73, 85; 7th Army 49
Usher, Plt Off Dennis 18–19, 22

Valentin, Lt Georges **61**, 61
Verrier, Sous-Lt Marcel 62
Vliet, Maj Corrie van 78

Waddy, Flt Lt John L **14**, 14, **4**(38, 90)
Wade, Wg Cdr Lance 'Wildcat' **20**, 20, 21, **36**, 65
Walker, Sqn Ldr James E 24, 28–29, 32, **16**(41, 91–92)
Warspite, HMS 51, 59
Webb, Sqn Ldr Paul **73**, 82
Webb, Sqn Ldr Richard 11, 17, **81**, 82
Wedgwood, Sqn Ldr Jeff H 7, 11, **12**, 12, 13, 15, 15, **3**(38, 89–90)
West, Flt Lt J G 'Shorty' **37**, 37, **22**(43, 92)
Westenra, Sqn Ldr Derek 'Jerry' 19, 63, 68
Whitamore, Sqn Ldr 'Babe' 13, 56
Wilmot, Lt Col Laurie 50, 57, 93
Wilson, Plt Off Alastair **10**, 15
Wilson, Flt Sgt 78
Winskill, Sqn Ldr Archie 29, **30**, 30, 32–33, 34
Woods, Sqn Ldr E N 'Timber' **27**(44, 93), **80**, 80, 81